"As someone who h Guryan Tighe's *Unmasking Fear* revolutionary in its approach to one of humanity's most fundamental challenges. Rather than offering simplistic strategies to 'overcome' fear, Tighe provides a sophisticated framework that transforms fear from obstacle to opportunity. Her three gateways of curiosity, gratitude, and purpose offer practical pathways that leaders at all levels can implement to create more authentic organizations and lives. This book brilliantly bridges personal development with collective transformation—exactly what our divided world needs. I will be recommending it to both my executive clients and university students as essential reading for anyone seeking to lead with greater purpose and authenticity."

—**Dr. Denise M. Lucy**, professor and executive director, Institute for Leadership Studies, Dominican University of California

"Wisdom for our times: Fear is one of the most misunderstood emotions, yet one of the most influential. *Unmasking Fear* is a guide to working with the energy of fear and using it as a catalyst for creating a better life, especially useful during this period of uncertainty. Using transformational practices and thought-provoking reflections, Guryan Tighe charts a pragmatic, comprehensive, and insightful path to developing greater agency in a changing world. For anyone in the grip of fear, or longing for deeper connection to themselves and others, this book will propel you towards greater clarity, confidence and peace."

—**Randy Taran**, author of *Emotional Advantage* and founder/CEO of Project Happiness.org

"Reframing our relationship with fear and looking for ways fear can benefit self-development would seem to be a high order of aspiration. Yet Guryan Tighe's revelatory work highlights how fear, though it can cripple, can also enlighten and be used as an ally and a tool to open doors to greater authenticity notwithstanding real and palpable terror. There is wisdom, light and candor in Tighe's analysis, distilled from a wide range of personal and professional experiences. She shows—no small feat—how fear, which can often hold us back, can also illuminate and liberate."

—**Michael Krasny, PhD,** author of *Off Mike, Spiritual Envy, Sound Ideas* and *Let There Be Laughter*

"For many of us, our internal fears and dialogues—both conscious and unconscious—hold us back from achieving our full potential. Guryan artfully unpacks the cause of these self-limitations using a combination of science, art, and empathy. She is an insightful guide to find what you want to be and how you want to show up in the world. She does this by teaching us how to confront our fears and truly listen to ourselves and others through practical interactive reflections, activities, and practices. A must read for anyone who wants to improve their life and reach their self-defined potential."

—**Josh Wright,** behavioral science expert and entrepreneur

UNMASKING FEAR

How Fears Are Our Gateways to Freedom

GURYAN TIGHE

Health Communications, Inc.
Mt. Pleasant, SC

www.hcibooks.com

Library of Congress Cataloging-in-Publication Data
is available through the Library of Congress

© 2025 Guryan Tighe

ISBN-13: 978-0-7573-2548-9 (Paperback)
ISBN-10: 0-7573-2548-3 (Paperback)
ISBN-13: 978-0-7573-2549-6 (ePub)
ISBN-10: 0-7573-2549-1 (ePub)

All rights reserved. Printed in the United States of America. No part of this publication may be reproduced, stored in a retrieval system, or transmitted in any form or by any means, electronic, mechanical, photocopying, recording, or otherwise, without the written permission of the publisher.

HCI, its logos, and marks are trademarks of Health Communications, Inc.

Publisher: Health Communications, Inc.
        1240 Winnowing Way, Suite 102
        Mt. Pleasant, SC 29466

Cover, interior design, and formatting by Larissa Hise Henoch

THIS IS
DEDICATED TO LUNA
FOR ALL OF IT . . .

To Rodger,
Here's to exploring
the gifts of fear..."

[signature]

CONTENTS

INTRODUCTION: A Gateway to Freedom | 1

PART 1: Let's Level Set | 7

CHAPTER 1: My Invitation to You | 9

CHAPTER 2: What Is Fear?
The Roles of Reacting and Responding | 17

CHAPTER 3: How Fear and Pain Are in Cahoots | 27

CHAPTER 4: Introduction to the Eight Basal Fears | 33

CHAPTER 5: What's Possible? | 47

PART 2: The Gateways | 59

CHAPTER 6: Practicing Your Practices | 61

CHAPTER 7: The Significance of Curiosity | 69

CHAPTER 8: The Power of Gratitude | 83

CHAPTER 9: The Role of Purpose | 93

PART 3: Your Assets | 113

CHAPTER 10: Self-Awareness: A Tool to Access Freedom | 115

CHAPTER 11: The Power of Pause | 133

CHAPTER 12: Body as Informer | 139

CHAPTER 13: The Influence of Storytelling | 153

PART 4: The Invitation | 161

CHAPTER 14: Your Unique Patterning | 163

CHAPTER 15: The Eight Basal Fears Revisited | 173

CHAPTER 16: Listen to Listen | 183

CHAPTER 17: Let's Close How We Began | 191

EPILOGUE: Not All Who Wander Are Lost | 199

Acknowledgments | 210

Notes | 212

About the Author | 213

A Note from the Illustrator | 215

INTRODUCTION

A GATEWAY TO FREEDOM

My name is Guryan Tighe. I refer to myself as a fear technician. I have spent eight years and approximately 8,000 hours coaching people about how to manage their fears. These conversations have taught me how fear impacts our decision-making. What commonalities do we all share? What elements differ for each of us? What happens if we learn to understand our fear? How can engaging fear differently—by getting curious as to the information it has for us rather than conquering or avoiding it—grant us access to more peace? If we write the story that fear is a teacher and not the enemy, we can create a safe way to explore the information it holds for us.

This book is a guide for intentional decision-making that's in support of your truth and your freedom. It will prepare you to face uncertainties and unknowns with curiosity and confidence and can connect you to your ultimate purpose. It contains methods, techniques, and practices that help you reframe your relationship with fear from a restrictive and unhealthy approach to a healthy one. There are stories about my personal experiences as a fear technician as well as case histories about my clients.

This book provides insights that will allow you to break free from unhealthy constructs and conditioning that are influencing your decision-making—sometimes, at a level you may not even be aware of. It will teach you how fear can be your informer. It will connect you to yourself more deeply and, in so doing, will connect you to others at greater depths than before.

From here, we can move from automatic reaction to intentional response. You get to make choices in your life that come from your truest self, choices that enable you to build the life you want.

This is a guide to your freedom and your purpose.

I've always been drawn to this work. My business has always been people. Prior to being a fear technician, I was a head of speaker development, and I can't tell you how much fear I witnessed, as most people have a fear of public speaking and often experience the imposter syndrome. I was also a chief culture officer, and I witnessed cultures of fear within the organization I worked for and with those I've partnered and led trainings for. I was also a partner in a strategic communications agency, and everything comes down to communication. But first we have to understand how we're communicating to ourselves. It's through this process that I realized fear has always been with me. In fact, I recently heard the phrase "all research is me-search." Perhaps that's what really led me to this work: finding a new relationship with fear so that I could navigate my life differently and share knowledge with you.

My intention in writing this book is to help people reframe their relationship with fear so that it becomes healthy and constructive. With my clients, I show up to each conversation with a student's mind, with curiosity and presence. What I share here is the cumulation of witnessing many people's stories: the experiences we as humans have with fear—a largely unexplored topic—and what we can learn from these experiences.

The time feels opportune as fear is rampant. And fear can be contagious. While fear in our world gets louder and louder, understanding our own relationship with fear feels like a worthwhile endeavor.

I am not devoid of fear. In fact, I believe that *we are our work*. I don't mean you're the job you do. I mean that which is wanting to be healed within us gives us the opportunity to work on it, if we so choose. Then we're able to share that work with others. As I said, it's not that I didn't and don't have fear. Fear was and is often with me. In my case, a healthy relationship with fear was calling me. Fear has been a long part of my journey, and while I still do have fear, it is a transformed relationship from where I once began.

One concept I spend a lot of time talking about with clients is understanding their *why*. Getting in touch with your own purpose and being able to articulate it to yourself clearly helps you stay true to that purpose. So, what's *my* ultimate why for helping you explore fear? Why is this work so important to me? It's my personal why: to help create a world of "and," not "or" (I come back to this in greater detail). It's to help you live the life you want to choose. To me, nothing is more sacred—or elusive—than choice. We're constantly bombarded with stimulus inputs, distractions, desires, frustrations, addictions, aversions, and yes, fears. All too often we're the victims of our own knee-jerk reactions to these inputs rather than actually giving ourselves the space—the *pause*—to choose how we want to respond. The good news is that amid all the static white noise of our day, our bodies, minds, and even our surroundings are constantly sending us clues to explore and cues to remind us of the choices we want to make. And fear—big, scary, impossible-to-ignore fear—is one of the most primal, useful, and misunderstood clues to who we really are and what we value most. So, by understanding fear—by unmasking it—we come face-to-face with our own deeper sense of purpose, identity, and most of all, choice.

Lastly, one of my favorite sayings is that your *why* is bigger than your *I*. I'm in service of something much bigger than myself. With that, none of what you are about to read is "mine." My intention is to help people reframe their relationships with fear to be healthy and constructive. As a result of my commitment to my intention, I believe I have been gifted access to this beautiful, universal wisdom. This wisdom is available to us all and speaks to the power of purpose, which we'll explore more. If I'm able to help even one person—possibly you—reframe their relationship with fear and make it an ally instead of an enemy, I will have aligned my intention in the truest possible way.

Before we start, I want to share something with you. I believe in what I call "ology." What does that mean? For me, it would be Guryanology. For my friend Alex, by way of example, it would be Alexology. For you, it would be *firstname*ology. Here's what ology is for me: As I read most books, I have a Sharpie and a highlighter. If information resonates with me, I keep it by highlighting it and beginning to practice the recommended behavior or mindset. Perhaps I shift my opinion as I gain information that I wasn't previously aware of, altering my perception about a matter. On the other hand, I don't want to miss out on gems of information because something written triggers me or doesn't fall in line with what I currently subscribe to. So, if language is used that sets me off for whatever reason, I might use a Sharpie to remove that particular element, without losing all of it. If there are things that resonate with me and serve who I am, I adopt them. This may include elements of Buddhism, Dagara, Sufism, mystery, science, Judaism, academia, and so on. And it doesn't mean I am any of these things singularly. If something you read resonates with you, keep it. If it doesn't, let it go and move on. Not every tool works for everyone. Make your own toolbox. Make it your ology.

What is possible? Simply put, our freedom. By having a greater connection to what is true for us, we can make integral choices that support our truth and express ourselves intentionally. This is an invitation to become unstuck.

Let's get started.

PART 1:

LET'S LEVEL SET

CHAPTER 1

MY INVITATION TO YOU

Fear is something we avoid experiencing because it's painful. It's also something we avoid talking about even though it has much information that can help us. Why? Because we fear fear, and we fear pain. What if it was possible to form a healthy relationship with fear? What if we were able to learn from our fear? What might happen if we approached fear with curiosity instead of trepidation?

REFRAMING OUR RELATIONSHIP WITH FEAR

Most of the language I've heard or read talks about being "fearless" or trying to "conquer fear." Easier said than done. When someone is angry, the worst thing we can say is "calm down." It's similar to fear. When someone is experiencing fear, telling them to calm down or just push through it is rarely a welcomed invitation. But what if, instead of being afraid, we could embrace our fear, seeking to understand and learn from it. *Embrace my fear?* you ask. That's absurd. But as absurd as it may sound, fear has a lot to teach us.

Governments, religions, and businesses have used fear to divide and control us. It's an incredibly effective way to make someone feel they need to do something. Take consumerism, for example. Many product sales are based on creating the fear that you're not enough and that you can fix not being enough by buying Product X.

Systemic fears can create constructs that many of us subscribe to, beginning at a young age. Take success. Have you asked yourself what success means to you? Are you working to build toward it? Many people haven't defined what success means for them—or even revisited the topic as they've navigated their life journey. We subconsciously adopt a vision of success, and then we start climbing up the ladder without even knowing if we want what's at the top. For instance, when I ask my clients this question of what success means to them, a very small percentage have an answer readily available. And when we start to explore the question, we discover that many initial answers aren't coming from their authentic truth. They come from constructs that exist around us. For instance, they might think success is a certain amount of wealth or income, or being employed by a specific brand or company name, but when we look deeper, we discover those might be small factors, and other important ones aren't being considered. These could include flexibility, autonomy, family, creative expression, and so forth. Many constructs can affect us: capitalism, family and cultural constructs, keeping up with the Joneses. . . . The opportunity is to begin to understand what is true for each of us. What is success for you?

What if we could turn toward fear with curiosity? What if we could understand those fears? Learn to listen to them? Learn from them and be at peace with them? All kinds of new possibilities open up.

FEAR'S CONNECTION TO AUTHENTICITY

As more choices open up, we get closer to our true purpose, which helps us to live more authentically. By exploring our fears and accessing greater authenticity within ourselves, we gain more confidence in who we are. An unintended (perhaps) generative outcome of this is allowing us to make space for others to be who they are, because being who we are authentically isn't challenged by external inputs or differences with other people. It comes from our own inner truth. Empathy not only becomes possible, it's a byproduct. *What divides us—fear—is then the bridge that unites us.*

I believe that fear is one of our greatest teachers. What an incredible asset we've been given—if we can shift our relationship to fear's presence and recognize the gems of wisdom it offers us. It may not sound easy, but I ask you: How easy is living under the grip of fear?

In my case, examining my fears allows me to stay curious, foster compassion, and promote

Fear is the flashlight to discovering our truest self.

feelings of courage. Understanding how fear can be an ally is important because the world is experiencing a lot of uncertainty and anxiety. This makes it a playground for our unexplored fears.

On a personal level, once we can learn from our fear, we discover that *what we fear is actually where we want to grow.* Think about it for a moment. We could be scared of everything. However, there are only a few things that each of us fear. Our fear is shining a light on the path we are called to walk down in order to become the newest and best version of ourselves. If you have a lot of fear about a possible move to a new city, quitting a job, or submitting a poem for a poetry slam, that's your fear telling you where you want to go.

On a macro level, we're facing climate change, AI uncertainty, racial injustice, generational shifts, and political divisiveness, to name just a few threats. Living with these issues leads to a heightened sense of anxiety. As a result, many people lose their ability to choose how they respond. They turn to instinctive, fear-based reactions that contribute to groupthink rooted in scarcity and, worse, mob mentality. In other words, fear can be contagious.

Many of us want to change, but we don't know how to effect it. All too often many of us feel just plain stuck. And that can be terrifying. When we feel stuck, it seems as though we're reacting unintentionally, making repeated unskillful decisions—and it can feel automatic, like we don't have a choice to engage differently. This is a result of an unexamined relationship with fear.

Fear often prevents people from making choices that reflect who we are—and discovering who we are is our true purpose. I find it remarkable that there are 8 billion people in the world, all with different fingerprints. We each have the ability to make our own impression. Being who we are is a purpose worth exploring. And what if a healthy relationship with our fear can lead us to who we truly are? To live life as our true self? As I often say to my clients, "Shift happens."

FEAR AND ZERO-SUM THINKING

Fear divides us, yet we all share it. I believe zero-sum thinking is at the core of this division, and exploring our fears becomes the anecdote to our zero-sum thinking.[1] The term is derived from game theory. Zero-sum thinking perceives situations as zero-sum games, where one person's gain results in another's loss. However, unlike the game theory concept, zero-sum thinking refers to a psychological construct—a person's subjective interpretation of a situation. Zero-sum thinking is captured by the saying, "Your gain is my loss" (or conversely, "Your loss is my gain").

It's worth taking a moment to put some clarity around what I mean by "why." When I refer to you or I having a *why*, I am referring to a North Star—a directing principle that serves as a compass, so that we live our purpose with intent, making decisions that support what we are in service to: in my case, helping create a world of "and," not "or." I am not referring to why from an excuse perspective, or a mindset of lack, which might sound like "Why bother?" or "Why me?" The power of why when used as a compass for purpose can continually remind us of how we want to engage the moment in which we find ourselves.

By way of example, a friend of mine went through acupuncture school, and the first few years were quite grueling—often requiring unrelenting focus and commitment. While it may have been enticing to dwell in a *Why am I even doing this?* mindset, what carried her through was a view of *Why am I doing this? What world can I make possible when I'm through this phase?* That's where she gets to be in service to others' healing and well-being, and that possible future propelled her through some challenging phases along the acupuncture school journey.

Why am I writing this book? My hope is twofold. I'd like you to have a healthy relationship with fear: one that informs you of your growth and what matters most to you. Unexplored fear can disconnect us from ourselves and one another. When we understand what fear is teaching us, we can increase our connection—to ourselves and others—by increasing our understanding. If we could understand others, perhaps some of the division might lessen.

> *The difference between a comedy and a tragedy is that in a comedy the characters figure out reality in time to do something about it.*
> —Bennett W. Goodspeed

And it's never felt more timely to understand what our fear is trying to teach us. We are the product of living within a systemic fear of scarcity. In the middle of 2025, we have found ourselves at the intersection of fear and peace. *When we are in fear, we give our power away.* If we let fear prevail, destruction reigns, disempowerment continues, and racism and subjugation of the disenfranchised continues unabated. We must turn into our fear to see what it is showing us. Peace, freedom, and integrity are at stake. The fear of scarcity, the suggestion there's not enough to go around, is self-defeating. We no longer have to accept a zero-sum game as the foundation of our system. In fact, we can't, because disconnection doesn't create a path forward for any generative community. Collectively, we all have the same fears. This becomes a way of understanding one another, perhaps even a way of uniting us.

We can choose to reframe our relationship with fear—to see our circumstances through a new perspective, to allow for other perspectives, to create win-win systems. We can do this if we so choose. Shall we build this bridge together?

What if we could shift our unintentional reaction to fear to an intentional response that benefits rather than hurts us? It's possible to escape from thinking and systems that don't serve us, to live in choice versus "shoulds," to have the freedom to be our authentic selves and express our truth—in other words, to live with purpose, to begin to free ourselves by using the very fears that hold us back. In so doing, we can create genuine community and connection through purpose.

So I ask you: What are you afraid of? Which of your choices are driven by fear? Just imagine what might happen if you approach your fears with courage. *With fear as our ally, choice becomes possible.*

Fear is courage unrealized.

To understand how fear plays out in our societies, we have to begin with our personal relationship to fear.

Are you ready to join me for this journey?

SEEDS TO PLANT

- What divides us—fear—is the bridge that unites us.
- What we fear is actually where we want to grow.
- When we're reacting mindlessly to fear, we're giving our power away.
- With fear as our ally, choice becomes possible.
- Discovering who we are is our true purpose.
- Fear is courage unrealized.
- Befriending fear is scary—and worth it.

CHAPTER 2

WHAT IS FEAR? THE ROLES OF REACTING AND RESPONDING

Always do what you're afraid to do.
—Ralph Emerson

I was scared of the dark. Not just as a young girl but as a grown woman. My ex-husband and I lived in a railroad apartment in San Francisco. He would often travel for work for a week or so. Our bedroom was at the end of a long hallway. It's rare when I don't have to get up to use the restroom in the middle of the night. When he first left, I would lie awake in bed weighing my odds. Do I go down the dark hallway and get murdered on my way to the bathroom? Or do I stay in bed and see if I can hold it in and make it back to sleep until morning light? For many nights I fought this battle, often not going, which had multiple downsides. The hardest part was sensing the power that fear had over me. So, one night, I accepted my fate. *I'm going to get murdered on my way to the bathroom.* So I slowly emerged from bed, opened the door, and began walking down the hallway. I walked, one step at a time, expecting the unavoidable. Then I made it. After relieving myself I got ready to return.

> *The power of fear was in its anticipation.*

Once again, I thought, *I'm going to be murdered on my way to the bedroom.* As I turned to the hallway and walked, one step at a time, I expected the unavoidable. But I made it!

I learned a lot about the anticipation of fear that day.

Once I moved into it, I could experience that my fear wasn't realized. What was giving it power was my putting life into the anticipation of it.

Fear is defined as a strong, unpleasant emotion caused by anticipation of awareness of danger. While this definition is accurate, I believe it's also limited because it doesn't distinguish between rational and irrational fear.

Fear gets a bad rap these days. In truth, it's a wonderful evolutionary gift that's greatly misunderstood. Fear is meant to protect us. Can you think of anything better at doing its job? This is the perfect response if we find ourselves in a situation where a rational fear is present. If a shark is chasing you, it's the fear that motivates you to swim faster or fight back and punch the shark hard on the nose. This is fear at its most useful, its most rational.

But another type of fear is irrational fear. For example, you're worried you may not know where you want to head (what to do next for your career, a move, a relationship, etc.), and as such, you're going to fail or lose out or be rejected. You might start sharing less about your confusion or uncertainty with others and disengage from them. Or you might constantly engage others in helping you figure out what to do and start driving others away. In this context, fear can drive you to make things worse for yourself. The trick is to know the difference between rational and irrational fear, and that takes work.

HOW DOES THE BRAIN RESPOND TO FEAR?

Our brain doesn't respond to irrational fear any differently than it responds to rational fears. We have to teach it otherwise. Rational fear lives in the present moment and helps us identify a threat to our survival. Irrational fear lives in the future. It's the what-if scenarios that keep us up at night. Further, rational fear drives us to connect with others. If your life was in danger, you would ask a stranger—even an adversary—for help. Irrational fear often causes us to isolate, withdraw, and disconnect from others.

In this book, I focus on how to have a healthy relationship with your irrational fears. The concepts I share do not apply to rational fear. Rational fear is meant to protect our safety and ensure our survival. This is why if we don't learn to have a healthy relationship with our irrational fears, our bodies will react the same way they do to rational fear, which removes us from being able to choose an intentional response. Moreover, given the current state of affairs, in certain circumstances, the line between irrational and rational fears has become thin, which is one of the reasons it's even more important to understand our relationship with our irrational fears.

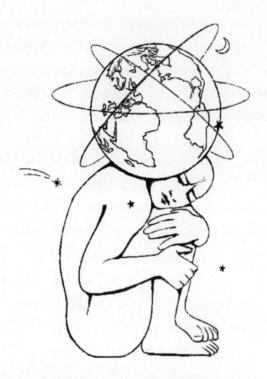

REACTIONS AND RESPONSES

Before we go further, I want to make a distinction about the language I use when speaking about reactions and responses related to fear. Psychologists define fear as a protective, primal emotion that evokes a biochemical and emotional response.[2] Fear alerts us to the presence of danger or the threat of harm, whether that danger is physical or psychological. While the biochemical changes that fear produces are universal, emotional responses are highly individual. When we perceive a threat, fear produces changes in our biochemistry and emotions on a subconscious level—what I refer to as "reactions"—whether that danger is actual or imagined. It's a natural, necessary, protective response, but when the reaction is out of proportion to the actual threat, it can be problematic.

I am very specific about the words "response" and "reaction." When I use the word "reaction," I am referring to an unconscious response. When I use the word "response," I am referring to a conscious response.

Reaction = Unconscious response

Response = Conscious response

Conscious responses reflect when we are choosing intentionally, so we won't be looking at these in detail. Rather we will focus on unconscious responses. Our reactions to fear are a universal function of our human brain makeup. Here are some of the truths. The amygdala is our fear center and is meant to protect us. It's the home of fight, flight, freeze, and fawn.

You may not have heard of fawning as a reaction to danger, though knowledge of it is growing in awareness. Licensed psychotherapist Pete Walker was credited with coining the term "fawning," in his book *Complex PTSD: From Surviving to Thriving.* Fawning is "a reaction to a threat by becoming more appealing to the threat."[3] Fawning refers to consistently abandoning your own needs to serve others to avoid conflict, criticism, or disapproval. Fawning is also called the "please and appease" reaction and is associated with people-pleasing and codependency.

But let's return to our brains. The amygdala also affects the hippocampus, which holds our memory storage. Think of a time when you saw someone feeling insecure (in fear) and having a hard time accessing their memory (which may have been you at times as well). This might happen when you get to the question-and-answer segment after giving an important presentation in front of key stakeholders, or on a first interview when someone is asking about a pivotal experience you had that contributed to your growth. When we come from a place of fear, our amygdala is in the driver's seat, bringing about paralysis and anxiety. When we're in a place of trust, our prefrontal cortex—the epicenter of curiosity, expression, decision-making, and connection—is in control, hence the importance of understanding the relationship we have with our fears and working to create a relationship that serves.

Our fear launches us into protective mode when it senses danger. For irrational fears, danger can be the unknown. What's incredible, however, is how that very fear is actually giving us information about where we want to go and what we want to look at. And the great news—which may not seem great the first time you hear it—is that our bodies have built-in reactions to handling danger. We have cues that serve as a sort of wake-up call that we're reacting from a place of fear.

Some common reactions to this danger, as mentioned earlier, can be identified as the fight, flight, freeze, and fawn reactions. When activated, the stress response can make you react in these ways:

1. You fight the threat.
2. You flee from the situation.
3. You freeze and stay in place.
4. You please and appease.

When we're engaging in any of these behaviors at times or circumstances when our actual survival is not at risk, we might be having an unconscious reaction to irrational fear. Beginning to understand the difference between rational and irrational fear is helpful. It can bring a sense of safety, because you understand that your survival is not at risk—though your psyche may feel like it is. With this sense of safety, you can turn toward the fear and—with tools and practices—help alleviate it and connect you to your freedom.

I want to take a quick moment to explain some of the tools in this book for you, before we jump into the first one. There will be areas called "reflection" and those called "practice" throughout. Reflections are opportunities to increase your self-awareness, to observe something about yourself and potentially learn about a new perspective or mindset. A "practice" is just that. An opportunity to practice a different behavior. It's not meant to be a one-time practice. If it resonates, it hopefully becomes one of many tools in your toolbox to support navigating a healthy relationship with fear.

> **PRACTICE**
> **ENGAGING YOUR FEAR**
> We've been trained to fear fear. If we desensitize this fear, a new world opens up.
> First, we ask ourselves . . .
> - *What am I afraid of?*
> - *Where am I feeling the most tension in my life?*
> - *Where do I feel stuck?*

Let's take the example of the imposter syndrome—a very common fear that people have. In our introductory call, I ask my clients what they want to get out of our work together professionally and personally. In response to professionally, the majority of the time, imposter syndrome is mentioned. It's that common. In psychology, the imposter syndrome is defined as a psychological pattern in which people doubt their accomplishments and have a persistent, often internalized fear of being exposed as a fraud. Generally, the imposter syndrome means we find ourselves in a new circumstance, one that might be inviting us out of our comfort zone: a definite playground for fear and a perfect example of what is calling for our attention.

One of my clients came to me concerned about feeling like an imposter when he was given a new project to lead. He described it as a fluster, and I asked him to elaborate. He said it felt like a number of things:

- I'm thinking about stuff and getting nowhere.
- I have ideas on where to start—but I'm too afraid to commit.
- If I do commit, I'm worried they won't like my idea.
- I feel like I need to get it right because I'm leading a team and don't want to cause thrashing.
- I feel like I have to do this all on my own.

Left unattended to, the imposter syndrome can have us focus on what we fear to be true rather than what is true, causing us to react, spin out, and feel flustered as this client put it.

I have my own experience with this. My very first job was with a PR agency. It was 2002, and I had to go through eleven interviews to get an entry-level account coordinator position. It was grueling. And the second I got it, I thought I had fooled them. I figured my congratulatory present to myself should serve a purpose. I purchased vanity glasses so that I would appear more intellectual. My logical reasoning (bargaining with myself) was that I would need them later in life, because everyone wears glasses later in life. My next move was to ensure that I presented myself as someone who had substance behind the look. In order to accomplish that, the only website I had open at all times was the thesaurus. I put everything I wrote through it to increase the level of sophistication and intelligence in my writing.

What was important about the imposter syndrome's presence was that it was telling me how important this job and delivering valuable and respected work was to me. Fear was encouraging me to stretch myself and learn new approaches, systems, ways of communicating, and so forth. If I had understood what fear was trying to show me, I could have taken the gifts without also criticizing myself every step of the way. We'll get into this more as we go. We can explore the information our fear has for us by creating a safe way to engage it—as our teacher, not the enemy. How can we begin to turn toward our fear?

Oh, I still have those eyeglass frames, and I haven't needed them yet.

SEEDS TO PLANT

- Fear is a wonderful evolutionary gift that's misunderstood.
- We can teach our brains to respond to irrational fears differently than rational fears.
- We can learn to move from unconscious reaction to deliberate response.
- Increasing our understanding also increases our safety to explore the information fear has for us.
- We can turn toward fear to reap the information it's making available to us.

CHAPTER 3

HOW FEAR AND PAIN ARE IN CAHOOTS

The things that frighten us just want to be held.
—Mark Nepo

We fear fear, and we fear pain. I have had thousands of conversations with clients over the years that have taught me about the relationship between fear and pain, and I have learned they are most certainly in cahoots. While it's not 100 percent of the time, most commonly the link between pain and fear begins quite early for us.

We experience a pain, which could include being teased on a school playground (feeling rejection), being sexually or physically abused (feeling worthless), or being left by a parent or loved one (feeling abandonment). What's more, we may not even recall the experience of pain. At that time, fear—your fierce protector—came in and said, "Hey, I'm going to make sure you never feel like this again.

I'm going to protect you from this pain. No matter what. Forever." Talk about fierce loyalty.

In the case of the schoolyard, maybe a bullied child stopped sharing their personality as brightly. Maybe the abused made themselves seem smaller. For the abandoned, perhaps they began doing anything and everything to prove they were worth staying for. At that moment in time, some of these behaviors may have been helpful—to stop the bullying, hide from the abuser, stay engaged in life. *The problem is, because we don't have a conscious relationship with our irrational fears, we don't know when this protective force is no longer needed.* When we are aware of irrational fears, we will be better equipped to determine if our old methods to protect ourselves are still relevant and supportive of who we are today.

THE NEUROSCIENCE OF DECISION-MAKING

Let's stop and take a look at the role of neuroscience and what's happening behind the scenes. Every time we make a decision, we're firing a neuron down a neural pathway. When we find ourselves in similar circumstances—making the same or similar decisions again and again—that neural pathway becomes what they call a superhighway. When we hear someone say, "This always happens to me," or we find ourselves in a circumstance that happens again and again—this is a clue that something worth examining is going on with our subconscious.

I want to pause for a moment for clarification. Because I use "clue" and "cue" throughout this book, I want to highlight what I mean by them. A "clue" refers to a chance to better understand something that is often a mystery while a "cue" refers to a thing we notice—often a signal from our bodies—that reminds us it's time to take action.

Our fear is fiercely dedicated to protecting us from pain, so without being aware, we react from a place of self-preservation. If we go back to the schoolyard example, maybe that child stays in the classroom during recess to avoid being teased or doesn't share an idea for a game—all because they're staying small to protect themselves. Fast-forward fifteen years and this might translate to silencing themselves in a corporate setting: "Don't invite me to brainstorm. I'm not an idea person. But when you have the idea, let me know, because I'm a get-it-done person."

When fear jumps in again and again to protect us from this pain, we create a habit—a superhighway. The downside is that the brain is no longer able to recognize there's a decision to be made. It's fired so many times in this direction, the activity in our brain becomes automatic (a reaction). Think of people talking about how hard habits are to break. They're hard to start too. Whether it's beginning a new gym routine or meditation practice, or going to sleep without scrolling on your phone, it takes time and commitment to establish a habit. Over time this becomes a pattern. If we have a behavior that isn't serving us that we've been practicing often because we fear pain and don't want that hurt to get triggered, we're going to react this way every single time we're in a similar situation—and by then we don't even have the choice to respond differently. Neuroscientist Norman Farb was interviewed on the podcast *Hidden Brain* in the episode "Changing Our Mental Maps," where he spoke to the role of default mode networks. One key element was how the brain's default mode network is essential to our survival but also can keep us stuck in rumination and overthinking. This underscores the importance of understanding when we're reacting—in default mode—and the importance of engaging our repetitive thoughts. After all, ruminating is not problem-solving.

FEAR AND PAIN ARE ON OUR SIDE

Remember that fear isn't doing this to harm you. Fear is actually on your side, trying to protect you. It may just be operating with some old information. *We stopped very early being in conversation with our fear, if we ever actually were. But it's not too late to start that conversation.* Maybe our fear was encouraging us to play clarinet (even if it wasn't the coolest instrument among our group of friends) or dance just for the sake of dancing because we felt like it (even if others didn't feel the same call). We can make the pain we can't get rid of our pathway to connection.

The pain that lingers within us is a signal that we still have something to heal, or we're not living our full self. If we take these two examples—if you never played the clarinet or stopped dancing—pain from not being able to express yourself will likely remain inside. If instead we connect to our pain, we can connect more deeply to ourselves—to wants and desires that we may have silenced, or to face issues we would rather resolve than continue to fear.

PRACTICE

Connecting to past pains might feel difficult as we often have done everything we can to avoid pain. Writing can be an accessible way to connect with emotions that might feel far off or challenging to reach. For now, we just want to acknowledge the pain that might be beneath the surface. This way, as we continue to explore the relationship between fear and pain, we have additional context to help us navigate.

Journal Exercise Prompts:

When I think back over the course of my life,

- These memories jump out as being hard (embarrassing, shameful, hurtful, etc.) for me. . . .
- I am still angry about . . .
- I feel unresolved about . . .

What's a prompt you can write for yourself?

We have the opportunity to engage our fear as an informer. When we can learn to understand the information that fear has for us, fear becomes one of our great teachers. To seek out this knowledge, we must first ask ourselves, *What is my relationship with my fears?*

SEEDS TO PLANT

- We fear fear, and we fear pain.
- We can be in conversation with our fears.
- When we are in this conversation, we can understand our protective patterns and their effects on our decision-making.
- Fears are often outdated protectors we don't need anymore–so learn from them, throw them a retirement party, and let them go.
- What once protected us may no longer as we evolve and grow.
- What is your fear really trying to tell you (besides "I'm scared")?

CHAPTER 4

INTRODUCTION TO THE EIGHT BASAL FEARS

Your pain is the breaking of the shell that encloses your understanding.

Even as the stone of the fruit must break, that its heart may stand in the sun, so must you know pain.

—Kahlil Gibran, *The Prophet*

Thousands of conversations about fear have given me insights into how to handle it. While specifics may differ, some themes are common. As you've read here, we tend to fear fear and pain. However, if we try to understand what lies beneath our fears, we can form a relationship with them.

We all share the same fears, which doesn't mean we all have exactly the same fears. My work has shown me that we all share the same core fears: what I call "basal fears," which brings us to the Eight Basal Fears. This is not to say everyone has all Eight Basal Fears. We each may have one or two. Many of our personal challenges and growth opportunities come back to our basal fears.

"Basal," as defined by Merriam-Webster, means "relating to, situated at, or forming the base." While details might be different—wanting to be accepted by peers, fearing first dates, desiring a parent's attention—my clients' stories displayed similar fears of rejection. By exploring the essence or the core of people's fears (low self-worth, fear of being oneself, etc.), we could get to their root cause (e.g., experiences, trauma, memories). We were then able to determine what formed the base of the fear. This work enabled me to identify the Eight Basal Fears that I believe we all share.

The Eight Basal Fears are fears regarding

1. Loss (letting go)
2. Rejection (not being liked or accepted, abandonment)
3. Loneliness and isolation
4. Self-worth (not being good enough, failure, inadequacy)
5. Authenticity (not being one's true self, fear of success)
6. Feeling lost or directionless (fear of the unknown)
7. Scarcity
8. Death and mortality (loss of self)

When we experience a fear, there can also be an unintentional closing or closing, or both. An unintentional opening occurs when, coming from a place of fear, we might do anything to protect ourselves from pain, including shutting down (leaving a circumstance, taking an avoidance nap, not sharing with others what we're navigating). These can serve as cues that remind us to wake up, reengage our conscious thoughts, make deliberate choices, and practice self-awareness. By learning to identify the signals and cues our body is sending us in various situations, the very act of *noticing* those cues can help increase our self-awareness and lead to a deeper understanding of how to stay in choice mode. We can ask ourselves—and as we practice the role of the observer (which we explore in chapter 10), we can witness—"Is this unintentional opening and/or closing a behavior I'm currently practicing?"

Because we have so much practice with allowing our self-critic to take over, we don't realize what we may be protecting. *A lot of our activity boils down to protecting ourselves from pain.* We fear pain and hurt because, as a society, we haven't been able to hold ourselves and one another in safe spaces to explore this pain, to have it, or to release it. As a result, at all costs we're going to fear pain and continue to avoid it. And fear is out to protect us from experiencing it.

In actuality, fear is a Band-Aid that's not going to fix the deeper wound, nor erase or eliminate the pain—even if it might feel like a temporary salve. Band-Aids need reapplication when the wound is opened again and again—yet underneath, the source of the wound remains, intensifying as it's left unattended. Think of fight, flight, freeze, or fawn, but to its worst extent. It's pretty detrimental to our health: physical, mental, emotional, and energetic.

WHAT'S BENEATH OUR SURFACE FEARS?

Surface fears stem from basal fears. But surface fears can help guide us to our basal fear(s), which may initially be hard to identify. You may need some time to discover your basal fear(s). When I'm working with a client, we'll get to a basal fear in time—unless they happen to be acutely aware of it, which some people are. First, we usually focus on daily challenges such as anxiety, a comparison mindset, or the imposter syndrome.

Understanding what is at the core—or what our basal fears might be—is a process. Think about it. Doctors ask, "How are you feeling today?" not "What's the core of your problem?" A close friend and thought partner of mine shared that with me when he suggested I warm people up to the idea of reframing their relationship with fear rather than diving in deep at minute ten. What a helpful tip it's been as I realize how scary exploring fear for most people can be.

One of the gifts of all my discussions about fear with my clients and companies I've worked with is to have been shown how similar our fears are. Let's look at them in more depth:

1. **Loss (letting go)**
   I can't live without _____ [fill in the blank].
   Unintentional Opening: *Therefore, I will create the illusion of control (hardship) for me to hang on to.*
   Unintentional Closing: *Therefore, I won't live.*

2. **Rejection (not being liked or accepted, abandonment)**
   I'm not good enough.
   Unintentional Opening: *Therefore, I will do anything to be accepted.*
   Unintentional Closing: *Therefore, I'm not going to try.*

3. **Loneliness and isolation (fear of being alone)**
   I'm all alone. I can't be alone.
   Unintentional Opening: *Therefore, I will attract anyone I can.*
   Unintentional Closing: *Therefore, I will stay in a bad situation.*

4. **Self-Worth (not being good enough, failure, inadequacy)**
   I'm not good enough / There's something wrong with me / I'll never get it.

   Unintentional Opening: *Therefore, I'll overextend.*

   Unintentional Closing: *Therefore, I'm stuck trying to compensate or medicate—or therefore, I'll shut down.*

5. **Authenticity (not being one's true self, fear of success)**
   I can't be true to myself and succeed at the same time.

   Unintentional Opening: *Therefore, I'll win at my own expense.*

   Unintentional Closing: *Therefore, I'll choose to lose.*

6. **Feeling lost or directionless (fear of the unknown)**
   I feel lost and I don't know where to go or what to do.

   Unintentional Opening: *Therefore, I do too much and get nowhere.*

   Unintentional Closing: *Therefore, I don't do anything (and keep suffering).*

7. **Scarcity (fear of not having enough)**
   There's not enough _____ [fill in the blank: love, money, time, willpower, etc.].

   Unintentional Opening: *Therefore, I'll do anything (violate my true being—my purpose) to get it.*

   Unintentional Closing: *Therefore, I'm stuck.*

8. **Death/Mortality (loss of self)**
   I'm afraid of dying (scarcity of time).

   Unintentional Opening: *Therefore, I will see death everywhere (empower my fears).*

   Unintentional Closing: *Therefore, I will see death nowhere.*

Unfortunately, there isn't a prescribed answer of what to do when you discover your basal fear(s). There isn't an algorithm to be fearless or rid yourself of past pain. However, fear is a doorway to seeing what shifts can be made. What pain is being protected? What can be released? By connecting with these truths, we can begin to create space so that we can connect to that which is truly important to us and the freedom to be who we truly are.

BASAL FEARS CAN SUPPORT US TO HEAL OUR PAIN

Given that I refer to myself as a fear technician, I'm often asked what my own primary basal fear is. For me, like many of us, it originated from a pivotal experience in my younger life. I was twelve years old. My brother was away at soccer camp. My parents had divorced a couple years prior, and my brother and I would go back and forth every other week to stay at each of our parents' places. Because my brother was away, I was staying at my dad's apartment alone on my own this particular week. I remember my dad coming home and sitting me down on the couch in the living room as he had something he needed to talk to me about. There were sliding glass doors behind him, so my visual was the silhouette of him. I'll never forget it.

I wouldn't call it pacing, but he was definitely walking back and forth. I could sense the heaviness of what was coming, even though I had no idea what it was about.

"Guryan, I won't be able to be your father anymore. I am ascending to the fifth dimension where I am going to become part of the white light. While I won't be your father anymore, I will be your spiritual guide."

He waited for my response. After a long pause I looked up at him. "Can I page you when you get there?"

This wasn't coming from a place of jest. I didn't understand what he had just told me, and pagers were, at that time, how we found each other when we weren't together to let the other know to call. He didn't understand my response, nor did he think it was funny. What followed is a little blurry to me, perhaps understandably so. What I remember is that he was disappointed in my reaction and left.

When he was gone, I called my mom to inform her that Dad was going to commit suicide. I was twelve. I heard "white light," and my mind wrote whatever story it could to make sense of the information I had just received. The next thing I knew, my mom and my uncle were there to take me, and my belongings, to my mom's.

I had an active imagination as a kid. My brother was a lot more literal, so when he returned home, my brother believed our dad—who informed him that I left to live with Mom full time without providing context as to why. My brother wouldn't see this side of my dad until about six years later when my father and his spiritual wife sent their wedding invitations stating that unseen beings would be officiating their ceremony. My dad later informed me that he didn't tell my brother but had told me because I was an old soul. I guess I hadn't attuned to that knowledge at twelve.

So began about a twenty-three-year stretch of being mostly estranged from my dad, save for a few extended family gatherings and some challenging altercations along the way. Not until my divorce would he and I begin anew.

So what's my basal fear? Lack of self-worth.

And just to make it slightly more complicated, my dad was the varsity girls' soccer coach at my high school. So over the following years, I would be walking down the hall to hear, "Guryan, your dad is the best!" only to know that I had been abandoned (from my perspective) by that very man.

Part of the shock of this circumstance was how incongruently my dad fathered. My childhood memories fell into the "I have the best dad ever" camp. He read to us every night before bed, taught us musical instruments, and played every sport imaginable with us across the street in the schoolyard after school let out. He was active. He was present. I felt loved.

Until I didn't. *If my dad didn't love me, how could another man? Was I worthy of love?* I began to think I wasn't. I began to believe—at least in this part of my life, as it relates to men—I wasn't enough. When the pain got lodged at age twelve, I would unknowingly begin the pattern of building toward my future stuckness. (The most common reason people come to me is that they feel stuck.) And from that moment on into adulthood I would continue to protect my twelve-year-old self, which I needed to do then but not in the decades that followed.

This was the story that my fear and anxiety began to run on a loop—to "protect" me from future pain of being left by a man again. Then my basal fear of abandonment manifested in my lacking self-worth. Thus would start my pattern of silencing my needs with men—anything to get them to stay. It became the basis of clouded judgment and a string of unhealthy decisions, mostly relating to men, through my life. In order to protect myself from the pain of being unworthy, I either had to overextend to prove my worth or accept whatever was offered, because deep down I didn't think I was enough.

This basal fear, my defender and protector, stayed on the front lines for years. No one informed my protector (because we fear fear and we fear pain) that she no longer had to protect me. In my relationships with men, I played out my wound again and again. Some of these men were good men, but not necessarily good for me with regard to the love I knew was possible and wanted. I related to love through abandonment. I would diminish my needs and make sure all of theirs were met until I had nothing left to give and I was a shell of myself. This continued until I became ready to decouple relating to love through abandonment. So I called it in again and again, because we are given lessons until we learn them. When I was ready—after peeling back multiple layers over the years—I broke that pattern and now I choose to practice connecting with love through the balance of giving and receiving. Now, in my relationships—familial, platonic, or romantic—if I notice myself silencing my needs, I pause. I lean in and speak to what I need. I make them aware of what is important to me and why—and then ask them directly for what I need. If they can't do so or aren't interested, in the case of platonic or romantic, I may choose to walk away from the relationship. In the case of familial—where walking away may not be as easy, I put boundaries in place to protect my well-being. I may not give as much of myself if my needs cannot be respected or met—and I can do so without judgment or story, because we all have different capabilities and are dealing with our own struggles, pain, and growth.

    A client of mine has fear of abandonment as one of her basal fears. Her parents left her with her grandparents for a year without saying goodbye and without communicating to her that they would return. Before age seven, she was mistreated and abused by her grandparents and parents and was even locked in the basement of a community school. As such, it's been a complicated relationship for her ever since with her parents, and there are times she chooses to set boundaries and cut contact off with them.

As a result of protecting herself from this pain, she developed a very close relationship with doubt over the years. When we looked at this fear, I had her finish the following sentence: "Doubt feels safe to me because . . ."

Doubt feels safe to me because it helps me avoid the impossible choice between my relationship with my parents (having a family at all) and myself. This protection created a misperceived sense of safety in doubt.

As she practiced doubt again and again over the years, we began to discover what else was true about doubt for her. We found that doubt kept her from vocalizing what she truly wants, so we created a new mantra that reflects the most current version of herself: "Doubt no longer serves as my safety—my truth is my new safety."

On a micro level, what these basal fears show us is what pain wants to be healed. And while we try to fill that void with external circumstances, it's not a sustainable approach. If our contentment is based on external circumstances, our contentment is based on external circumstances. When we have the knowledge of what is causing us a mindset of lack, engaging that very mindset becomes possible.

There is a way to reunite with your younger self who might still be protecting you. I, and many of my clients, have been able to do so through a writing exercise.

PRACTICE

Write a thank-you letter to my _____-year-old self.
Tell my younger self I'm sorry you had to go through it.
You didn't deserve it.
No one does.
Thank you for protecting me.
Let me share with you who I am now. [Share who you are, what you've accomplished.]
You don't need to protect me anymore.
You can let go. You must be exhausted. Let me take the reins.
Come, walk with me. . . .

I'll share mine with you.

Dear Twelve-Year-Old Guryan,

I remember so clearly. Sitting on the couch, Dad pacing back and forth—his silhouette pronounced with the backlit sliding glass doors behind him. Your fear. Your confusion. Your aloneness. I am sorry you had to experience that moment. Those words. I'm sorry you had to try to make sense of such a selfish act and that you took on any fault, blame, or ownership for his choices. You didn't deserve that. You only deserved love. You didn't deserve to be abandoned by your father "in secret"—since he didn't communicate this same truth to your brothers. You were twelve. Full of life and heart. You didn't deserve to be expected to understand. You didn't deserve to walk the halls of your high school being told what an incredible dad you

had–while he coached the girls' varsity soccer team.
You didn't deserve to be left and told over the years that you were in fact the one who left–since you moved to Mom's.
You didn't deserve to be less-than'd by this pivotal male figure. You didn't deserve all the pain and fear this brought you. It makes sense you never wanted to feel this way again, to never be left by another male, to not have to experience the pain and confusion and fear again. You did nothing to deserve it. It's not your fault. You are not to blame.

And you are, in great part, what has made me who I am today. I have committed myself to my journey of growth and healing. To knowing who I am. To continually discovering the next version of myself. To loving fiercely–without abandonment. I am surrounded by an incredible community and loved ones who are committed to being their best selves and who love me. What did we do with that fear? I built my own business focused on it. We created an approach that helps myself and others form a relationship with it that's healthy. That enables choice.

I lead with my heart. I walk with integrity. I have standards. I am continually learning to be more love. I allow nature to fill, nourish, and humble me. I create.

My heart is expanding now as I come for you. You have influenced the strong, beautiful, courageous, worthy woman I have become. Thank you.

This is an important time and these are important crossroads. I am ready to move forward with you. You don't *have to hold onto this anymore. You've carried this for thirty years. You don't have to protect me anymore. I am ready to take my power back from the men who have been in my life. To stand in all of my power with the future men who come in (in all forms). I am worthy of my worth. I forgive myself. I accept myself. I love myself just as I am.*

Come . . . walk with me.

Love,

Guryan

HOW BASAL FEARS PLAY OUT IN THE MACRO

We are living in interesting times, to put it mildly—where fears have been exposed more than ever, at least in my lifetime. Fear has been and is being used by governments, religions, and businesses to divide us. Fear is free. Fear can be monetized. And it can be used to target one's lack of worth. Any product or service from religion to the military to what's available on the grocery store shelves can be positioned to fill up the holes in your life and *fix* you. If you have *x*, we have *y* to grant the desired outcome you seek—your sense of worth. It's one of the most abused powers throughout history. People in fear give away their power, moving out of choice and into conformity with a narrative that may not be true for them or in their or humanity's best interest. Unexplored fear silences truth and solidifies extreme positions.

Our basal fear hasn't only been reinforced through our micro experiences in life. It is reinforced daily through macro experiences as well. If someone has the basal fear of rejection and will do anything to be accepted, they may fall victim to marketing about what they need to feel sexy (a certain hairstyle, a particular brand of clothing, an activity they need to be seen doing). It isn't unheard of to fill a void with consumption. But none of these actions are actually filling the void, and they can become self-fulfilling prophecies if there's a misperception that the void can be filled with a product or experience. All the more reason our awareness needs to be paramount, so that we can understand how fear is showing up and being used, and for whose benefit. We live with a systemic fear of scarcity. Systems and power benefit from it; we do not. As a result, we have overindulged in a mindset of lack-based thinking.

Communities are based on commonalities. If we begin to see the fears and pain beneath all our actions, we might begin to see one another. Our stories may be different, but the themes are similar. Fear can be the ultimate equalizer, a bridge to empathy and connection. Our basal fears can be a unifying bridge, a tool for compassion and understanding, a way to be in conversation with ourselves and one another.

SEEDS TO PLANT

- We haven't been taught how to safely have our pain—nor how to hold others in theirs.
- What if you could look at fear with levity? *You again?*
- Laughing at fear dispels the power it has over us, leaving behind only the lessons it is trying to teach us.
- If contentment is based on external circumstances, contentment is based on external circumstances.
- It's time to take back our power. Fear doesn't need to divide us. What if it's the bridge that unites us?

CHAPTER 5

WHAT'S POSSIBLE?

*Everyone thinks of changing
the world, but no one thinks of
changing himself.*

—Leo Tolstoy

A key element in reframing our relationship with fear is opening to the possibility that fear can serve as a door opener for us. It can connect us to truths (sometimes hard ones) we may not be consciously aware of and to critical information we need to inform how our decisions align with what it really is we want. Misunderstood and unexplored, fear impedes our ability to make an intentional choice by replacing those moments with automatic reactions. Fear isn't the end point. It's the door opener. It's about what's possible when we engage our fears rather than avoid them.

THE CONNECTION BETWEEN FEAR AND INTEGRITY

What is possible? Simply put, our freedom. By having a greater connection to what is true for us, such as the importance of expressing oneself artistically, we can make integral choices. One of my clients created a yearly planner and put it on the market for people to purchase. Another client submitted a piece of art to a local fair. Both actions support the truth that we can express ourselves intentionally.

It's challenging enough to maintain our integrity. Add the fear of unknowns on top and it's almost impossible. Our brain perceives uncertainty as a threat, which puts us in a state of fear. *Fear impedes our ability to make an intentional choice by replacing it with an automatic reaction.* Fear can undermine our integrity by forcing us to make inauthentic choices. There is no greater freedom than being yourself, and integrity can serve as a great barometer of your expression of self. Are you who you say you are? Do you live practices and behaviors that support it? Does your walk align with your talk? Integrity is a valuable trait in individuals—one that's being challenged as our environment changes around us, as truth itself is being challenged. We find ourselves more and more often in volatile environments. We don't know what will happen next week, let alone next year. And uncertainty takes up a lot of space and energy, impacting our decision-making ability and our connection to ourselves and others.

In short, it's hard to have integrity when you feel like you may not know what's around the corner. And yet, without it, we're prevented from being the truest version of ourselves. Communication can become confusing or misleading—causing increased separation and division.

Integrity takes courage, which demands a lot of us. It asks for our self-awareness and our curiosity, our ownership of our feelings and admission of our blind spots, our vulnerability and our strength. Our search for integrity drives us, whether we are aware of it or not, because what we're searching for is our truth. When integrity is absent, we can't see all our options, and our choices can lead to unintended consequences.

How does integrity require our vulnerability? When we do what we say and say what we mean, we are exposing our authentic selves and values to others. In doing so, we open ourselves up to rejection and failure. Whether we are communicating with loved ones, coworkers, or acquaintances, integrity is a cornerstone of connection. But achieving true integrity is a lot harder than it sounds.

Courage is the ability to do something even when it feels scary.

As we've seen, fear is meant to protect us. Our fear launches us into protective mode when it senses danger. Unknowns, therefore, equate to the need for protection. Given how many unknowns we face, that's a big playground for fear to have even more practice to become better at its job. However, if we begin to engage fear differently, we can discover that it holds keys to unlocking more of our truth.

What if our fears and doubts were access points to clarity and intentional decision-making rather than being barriers?

FEAR AS AN ACCESS POINT TO OUR FREEDOM

Without having a way of engaging them, our fears can make us feel stuck. But what if fear was an access point to our freedom? To greater conviction? What's possible from there? Let's take a deeper look at the intersection of fear and courage. I've worked with many people who have made the bold decision to leave a job that was not bringing them contentment—without knowing if their new role would be better. Some left jobs without having another job to go to. What initially kept them stuck in their original jobs was fear. What helped them make the decision to do the very thing they feared? Their courage.

Think about a courageous decision you made. What was happening immediately before you stepped into your courage? I'm guessing you were in fear. If you think about it from a danger response, the fear had you paralyzed, stagnant—most likely holding your breath. When moving into your courage, you exhaled, inhaled, and proceeded into that very energy from a different perspective. What if fear and courage are two sides of the same coin? Rather than either/or, consider a spectrum of wholeness on which courage and fear appear. You don't have to leap into your courage. You can begin to move closer by engaging your fear in a safe way and disarming it of its irrational power.

Moreover, fear may be present while we're being courageous. You can have fear and be courageous at the same time. In fact, we often feel more than one thing at once. Take leaving a job as an example. We can simultaneously feel excited and nervous about the change. Part of the zero-sum, win-lose mindset is binary thinking, which limits us greatly, forcing us to make up a story that we have to be excited or it's not really what we want. Or we're nervous because maybe we won't make it in the new role—another opportunity for the imposter syndrome to present itself. We don't have to be this *or* that. We can be this *and* that. Instead, we can be excited about the new opportunity that awaits us and nervous because some unknowns ask us to grow and stretch.

Fear can be the flashlight that illuminates our courage. Fear then reveals our deepest values—personal expression, contentment, family, our participation in some purpose that's bigger than ourselves, and so on. By mining our fears, we can connect to our purpose (what's most important, who we truly are, what cause we can serve).

> *Courage isn't the absence of fear. It's actually the ability to do something that frightens us.*

PRACTICE

If fear and courage are sides of the same coin, what if we could try on seeing the perspective of each?

Reflect back on a decision you made that asked for your courage.

- Was fear present before? If so, what did it sound like? What story was it telling you?
- What did your courage sound like? What did it enable you to do?

Think of a circumstance that you currently have fear about.

- Play out: What does the fear sound like? What story is it telling you?
- Play out: What does the courage sound like? What story is it telling you?

You don't have to act on either. For now, we're just exploring how close they are to each other and how different they sound.

Let me give you an example. A friend and thought partner of mine and I occasionally co-facilitate a workshop called "FEAR + PLAY: Activating Courage and Aliveness Through Experiential Connection." As I focus my work on fear, she focuses hers on the power of play. We bring them together as they're a powerful combination. She brings many assets and skills from improv into our workshops. One exercise is called "I Could Tell You a Story." We ask participants to tell us a story about fear and a story about courage—not the actual story, just what the story would be about. For instance, we've had participants tell us, "I could tell you a story about fear when I decided to leave my job for nothing." "I could tell you a story about courage when I moved from St. Louis to San Diego without knowing anyone." No matter how many workshops we ran, no matter how many people we heard from, fear and courage were always two separate stories. My co-facilitator would always call on me to share last. I would share the following: "I could tell you a story about fear when I decided to leave my marriage and go out on my own. I could tell you a story about courage when I decided to leave my marriage and go out on my own."

They both brought me fear—and they both asked for my courage.

Here's another example of how our fear is asking us to apply our courage. This is from a friend of mine who agreed to allow me to coach her through her fear of driving. She was in an abusive marriage and her now ex-husband had instilled a fear of driving in her to make her more reliant on him. This is her account of the process we moved through:

> I was in a horribly abusive marriage and quite literally did not know how to leave. Many people don't leave bad marriages because of the fear of being alone, but this was not my case. I was already lonely in my marriage and doing everything alone: physically, spiritually, and emotionally. Being alone was not a fear I could relate to. My fear was driving.
> I'll explain.
> Over the course of twenty years, my husband had convinced me I couldn't drive. He drove me everywhere. To my work, the grocery store, anywhere I or we were going. He convinced me I hated to drive, in order to restrict my movement—which, over time, became a story I adopted as true. It is worth mentioning

that I received my driver's license over twenty years prior and had driven without a problem.

Guryan came to visit, and he suggested I "borrow" my own sports car so we could go to lunch. I was frozen. Guryan offered to drive us. She asked me why I wasn't able to drive. I told her I hated it and no longer felt I knew how to. She asked if I could perhaps start by driving in the local neighborhood to "get used" to driving again. After she left, I took up the challenge and the first time I sat in my car by myself, I broke into tears. Actually, it was more like wailing. I realized I didn't know where the windshield wipers were or even the lights.

In time, I started driving my son to school but couldn't get on the highway. And then Guryan asked me, "When will you know you are ready to get on the highway if you don't try?" Those words once again challenged me, and I realized I had to. So, I got on the highway. I gripped the steering wheel so tight, it left marks on my palms. I exited as fast as I could at the very next off-ramp, then went back on again for a second try before my shoulders started to hurt with tension.

That evening, I called Guryan, giddy as a child. "Oh my god, I got on the highway," I shrieked. She cheered me on, and I gained even more confidence—the confidence I needed to leave my abusive marriage. This might sound silly to some, but the realization that I stayed in a bad marriage because he drove me everywhere and I was afraid of driving was real in my world at the time, and looking back now, I can't begin to imagine what that fear did to twenty years of my life.

"When will you know you are ready to retire the old story of 'I can't drive'?" was the next question Guryan asked me as we were catching up one evening. That weekend, I had to drive somewhere that required me to be on the highway for forty-five minutes. Once I arrived, I parked my car and cried. I had arrived safely. I remember thinking, What was I afraid of? Was that fear even real? I drove back home and once again called Guryan to tell her I had spent forty-five excruciating minutes on the highway. She cheered me on and reminded me that fear was designed to help you move forward, not back. These words were a seminal moment in my life and saved my life.

The night before I moved out of my home, Guryan made me a Spotify list and told me to play the music as I drove to the newest chapter of my life and think of it as my "freedom ride." The next morning, I packed my toddler in the car, took my dog, and said a prayer. I then embarked on my freedom ride. Never have I ever felt so free, so exhilarated. It was an indescribable feeling. We reached our destination safe and sound and it was not until the next day when I realized, *Wait a minute. I drove for hours on the highway!* And it was actually great. It's easier to drive on the freeways than in the neighborhood. As we parked in front of our new house, my three-year-old gave me a high five and said, "Mama, we did it!" And you guessed it, again . . . I cried.

One of the ways we can define fear is our core technique for staying alive in the face of threat. I told myself I was "staying alive" by avoiding freedom of movement, yet the truth is I was dying inside, one day at a time. I have since left my abusive marriage and cannot begin to tell you how free I am.

The next time Guryan came to visit, I picked her up and dropped her off at one of the busiest airports in the world, seamlessly navigating the traffic, and she could not believe that it was me. I had to remind her: I was actually a good driver before the crippling fear checked in and convinced me otherwise.

Let's take a look at this experience to see what was happening for my friend as she shifted her relationship with fear through this process. First, she established a pattern of not driving. In this case, her husband had instilled the fear, but her repeating the story again and again that she couldn't drive instilled the fable as her own. My being there and asking her about her driving brought a spotlight to her lack of freedom—and that she felt stuck in her marriage. She then connected to what was most important: that she didn't have her freedom. Rather than resisting the pain, she turned toward it. She allowed the tears and the wailing. She was then able to begin to create new neural pathways by beginning to drive, starting in what felt like a safer environments her neighborhood. The highway was going to ask her for courage—exactly where her fear was pointing her. When she was able to break down what was true (she didn't want to stay in her marriage) and what she was telling herself was true (she couldn't drive), she could take the steps necessary to disprove the story that was keeping her stuck in her marriage. Fear was showing her where she wanted to grow—which she emphasized by highlighting that fear is designed to help you move forward, not back. When she connected to her true pain—that she was dying inside staying in this circumstance—and turned toward her fear, it gave her the keys to her exit. I have goose bumps recalling it all, as courage is that humbling.

Irrational fear dissolves through recognition. The darkness of irrational fear can be a mirage. What happens to darkness when you shine a light on it? Like a magic trick, it loses power once you understand how the trick works. The power of naming is an incredibly valuable tool to lessen the grasp fear may have on you.

When we reframe our relationship with fear, we can embrace our fear for its knowledge as an ally rather than fear it as an enemy. When we use (not lose or conquer) our fear, we have freedom.

F—Facing
E—Expectations
A—Allows
R—Release

So let's dive in. This might be a little messy. Life can be messy. Fear and pain can definitely create a mess. What if instead we invite the mess in, in service of our freedom?

SEEDS TO PLANT

- Integrity takes courage.
- We are searching for our own truth–who we are.
- Without a healthy relationship with our fear, we
  - Make choices that are inauthentic.
  - React automatically from protective patterning.
  - Feel stuck.
  - End up wondering why in the world we just made the same mistake again.
- Fear becomes our flashlight to illuminate our courage.
- Our fears can lead us to connection with self and others.

PART 2:

THE GATEWAYS

CHAPTER 6

PRACTICING YOUR PRACTICES

We are what we repeatedly do.
—Will Durant

We are what we practice, and we're practicing something all the time. The more we practice something, the more "habitized" it becomes: mental agility, physical agility, resilience, patience, and so on. And like many things, x often begets more x. Every thought we have, every statement we make, every action we take, we are practicing something. The same notion applies to choice. We might be practicing self-limiting thoughts, or we might be practicing beneficial thinking. The words we use and the thoughts we have create our realities. We are practicing all the time. Given this, it seems worthy of bringing our attention to what "it" is we are practicing.

Where do we begin?
The only place we have the ability to change.
With self.

HOW PRACTICED IS YOUR SELF-CRITIC?

My own journey of self-exploration began after I left my ten-year marriage and was living on my own in San Francisco. It's kind of impossible to evaluate one area in your life that isn't "working" and not look at all the other areas of your life. It wasn't long after leaving my marriage that I realized I also had to leave my job as the culture was quite toxic where I was working. I thought that creating space in my life would connect me to the answer I was seeking. If I could just create space, new (job, partner, friends, alignment) would enter.

I discovered that within the space was just more space. It felt like a dark rabbit hole. When I would try to get out of my head and access some reprieve from self-doubt (a mask of fear), I often walked along Crissy Field out to the Golden Gate Bridge, taking solace in the cleansing air blowing off the bay. One day while I was walking, beating myself up mentally, as was a frequent occurrence at this time, I literally stopped myself in my tracks. I heard myself say out loud, "Guryan, if any of your friends talked to you the way you talk to you, you'd punch them in the face." So that day, I decided to name her. Who? My self-critic. I needed it to start with a G because she was still me, only she had a different vibe. I landed on Gretchen. (It's not that Gretchen is a bad name. I just happened to know a Gretchen who bullied me when I was young, so it felt appropriate.)

I was amazed by the frequency of Gretchen's presence in my life, the viciousness of her criticisms, and her tireless commitment to bring me down and make me less than. I guess in some way, her tenacity was almost commendable.

By naming her Gretchen, I gave myself the ability to observe her—to see when she came around, what settings I was in, who I was with, what I was engaging with, or what I was not engaging with. She was using a silent and deafening megaphone in my ear through self-doubt. From the role of the observer, I could begin to notice and engage with my thoughts rather than be victim to them.

I guess, like Alice's fall down the rabbit hole, it began my quest to truly discover who I was and whose thoughts were on repeat in my mind, because I was starting to realize they weren't all mine.

THE GIFTS OF THE SELF-CRITIC

As our relationship with fear can be a little complex until we have more practice engaging it for information, our relationship with our critic can also be complex at first. Gretchen is not a solely negative entity for me. She's trying to make me aware of something. *The critic is not a terrible thing. It might even have relevant information for us—just not when it's playing on loop ad nauseam.* What we want to do is mine the information it has; maybe it's telling us to be more detailed or to check in on a grandmother. It can have a lot of information, but if "I'm a terrible granddaughter" is what I'm repeating on a loop, that's not really leveraging the important nugget of the critical thought, which is that I want to set aside intentional time to call my grandmother and have an uninterrupted conversation.

Remember the new acronym for FEAR: Facing Expectations Allows Release? Recognizing fear, naming it, and counterprogramming it are all incredibly helpful. Unfortunately, so many of us fear fear to a level that we're wired to turn away from it the moment we sense it, to hide from it. We can't even turn to look at it. Recognizing it's there and naming it are really important tools to help dissolve the initial fight-flight-freeze-or-fawn reaction. This is why naming Gretchen was so powerful. It gave me the ability to notice when she was coming, to identify her playgrounds, and to see what information she had for me. Naming our fear gives us the ability to pause so that we can begin to break down the pattern, which initially might be our automatic turn away from fear.

> ## REFLECTION
> ## WHAT IS YOUR PREDOMINANT FEAR REACTION?
>
> While each of us may practice all of the fear reactions in different circumstances, it is typical to have a predominant reaction. When we know what our primary reaction is, we can begin to become aware of its presence and learn how to build responses instead of reactions.
> - Do you fight the threat (become combative, get heated, yell)?
> - Do you flee from the situation (detach, compartmentalize, dissociate)?
> - Do you freeze and stay in place (avoid, ignore, employ tunnel vision)?
> - Do you please and appease (silence your voice or needs, overextend yourself for others)?

We can either react to it unconsciously or respond to it consciously. And we often become our own worst enemies when we don't take the time to listen to what fear has to teach us. If we could begin to form a healthy relationship with our fear and listen to it, we could choose our response rather than have knee-jerk reactions dictate what happens next.

Fear is not the enemy. Fear is data.

Unlearning and learning can happen at the same time. What's more, they inform each other. In order to build new habits that promote intentional growth, we have to unlearn which patterns may be preventing us from recognizing our choice points.

We have to choose practices that support us. Then we have to practice them. Again and again and again.

PRACTICE

In order to keep ourselves accountable to our practices, we can reflect at the end of the day to recognize behavior shifts we're making and see where we would still benefit from doing so. At the close of your day or evening, take stock of your choices.

Five-minute journal exercise:
- Did I notice my fear today?
- Did I practice engaging my fear today?
- Did my fear have any information for me?

It may not be relevant every day, but for the days it is, this is an effective way to be aware of your progress on ensuring you have a healthy relationship with your fear.

What enables us to look at our fear instead of being plagued by it? We explore three gateways here: curiosity, gratitude, and purpose (service).

SEEDS TO PLANT

- We are what we practice, and we're practicing something all the time.
- The critic has information for us—if we can mine it for its value.
- Irrational fear dissolves through recognition.
- Fear is not the enemy—fear is data.
- Unlearning and learning can happen at the same time.
- Our fear may want us to be afraid of it—but our truth (and intuition) are wanting us to listen to it.

CHAPTER 7

THE SIGNIFICANCE OF CURIOSITY

Let your curiosity be greater than your fear.
—Pema Chodron

Reframing our relationship with fear may feel like a big undertaking. What if we think of it as an exploration? Where to begin? Let's start where most explorations begin: with curiosity.

When we bring our curiosity to the present moment, we can gain further access to our truth. The words we speak and the thoughts we have create our reality. What if we get curious about the words and thoughts we're using? And at what level of frequency?

Furthermore, when we practice curiosity, our brain activity is in our prefrontal cortex. The prefrontal cortex, as a reminder, is the home of curiosity, expression, decision-making and connection. If we are practicing an irrational fear (a story) and are in our amygdala —the fear center in our brain—we can neurologically shift into our prefrontal cortex by practicing curiosity.

By engaging our curiosity, we can remove judgment, assumption, and story creation. As irrational fears live in the future tense, they're just what-ifs, stories we create, assumptions we often make from a mindset of lack. When we give away our power to the story, we disconnect ourselves from our truth.

Let's revisit that client of mine who created and brought to market the planner she designed. Just before it was time to launch her product, her fear began to grow louder. She began to tell herself stories rooted in her fear of what-ifs. *What if I have gotten in over my head? I'm so busy with my full-time job—do I really need a side hustle? What if this totally fails and I've made a fool of myself?* When she removed the story creation and turned toward curiosity—she discovered why it was worth it. Creating this planner gave her a lot of energy, it was fun, and she looked forward to it. It was helpful for her as it was more than an average planner. It included space for self-reflection and guidance for connection to values to live intentionally, so she was also creating something that helped her in her growth process and she could now offer it to the world.

In order to make fear our ally, we must increase our understanding of the role it plays in our decision-making and our relationship with it. Remember, fear's only job is to protect us. Its role is keeping us safe. From fear's perspective, you're safe as the version of yourself you are—in your comfort zone, even if you feel stuck. This underscores the importance of seeing the irony in fear. What we're afraid of is exactly where we want to grow.

How can your curiosity help close the gap between the story and the information you're seeking? If fear is a future-tense story, then it's showing us there's something we don't yet know, something we might need more information about. Notice any questions you have, or ask yourself where you would like more information. In order to explore this, first we want to start to notice when fear is present.

IS FEAR HERE?

There are many ways fear might be alerting us that we are experiencing it: holding our breath, avoiding a conversation, taking what one of my clients refers to as "avoidance naps," and so on. By better understanding our relationship between any of these feelings and fear, we can make choices about our relationship with each and make more intentional decisions. *We fear because we believe something we value deeply may be in danger,* something we care deeply about is being threatened.

Fear is not an isolated emotion. We associate it with other experiences. Even if we're unaware of our own fear and the impact it's having on our decisions, there are other masks for fear: emotions we are more aware of (and in some cases, that are easier to experience) —that are closely connected with fear—sometimes serving as a mask for it. Common masks for fear include anxiety, insecurity, sorrow, shame, anger, comparison, and competition. These masks may serve as trigger points and are a clue that there may be a fear to explore. The fear exists beneath the mask. In a way, the masks can distract us from having to face the underlying fear that the mask is protecting.

Consider the story Thich Nhat Hanh tells about anger in his book *Teachings on Love.*

> A monk decides to meditate alone. Away from his monastery, he takes a boat and goes to the middle of the lake, closes his eyes, and begins to meditate. After a few hours of unperturbed silence, he suddenly feels the blow of another boat hitting his.

> With his eyes still closed, he feels his anger rising and, when he opens his eyes, he is ready to shout at the boatman who dared to disturb his meditation. But when he opened his eyes, he saw that it was an empty boat, not tied up, floating in the middle of the lake.... At that moment, the monk achieves self-realization and understands the anger is within him; it simply needs to hit an external object to provoke it. After that, whenever he meets someone who irritates or provokes his anger, he remembers: the other person is just an empty boat. Anger is inside me.

The invitation here is to see what information anger has for us. As this story shows us, it may not be in what triggered the anger but rather where the anger is coming from (within). Anger is not a negative or bad emotion. Neither is guilt nor sadness nor any of the other masks or perceived negative emotions. What we do with them may not be beneficial to ourselves or others. However, if we engage them, they become door openers. They are informers. *What is being triggered? And how is it manifested (fight, flight, freeze, fawn)? What am I protecting? What pain is buried within me that I can learn from? What is stuck within me? What can I release?*

REFLECTION

To leverage the masks of fear as entry points to more critical information that we might be avoiding, we want to get beneath the mask to understand the essence of the matter or what is most important. Use a journal to help you notice and unpack what is going on when you get angry. Try this when you notice if you're experiencing one of the masks for fear: anxiety, insecurity, sorrow, shame, anger, comparison, and competition.

First, identify your cues (before they turn into a reaction—outburst).

Then, create the *pause*.

Finally, practice curiosity to see what's beneath the mask.

Here's an example using one of my client's experiences with "learning from my anger":

Identify your cues:
- Feel aggression
- Feel tighter
- Start thinking/talking/acting faster
- Tone of voice gets forceful
- What other specific cues can you think of?

As soon as you notice your cues, create the *pause*:
- What's beneath the anger?
- What am I protecting?
- What am I scared is being threatened?
- What am I hurt by?

What else comes up for you as you engage your curiosity?

Anger, writes psychotherapist Robert Augustus Masters in his book *Spiritual Bypassing*, is "the primary emotional state that functions to uphold our boundaries. When we feel anger, it's an indication that something is wrong—a boundary has been crossed or a need is not being met. It's not always just about our individual selves, either—anger is an appropriate response to oppression." When we sense our anger, it is a clue to get curious: Has a boundary of ours been crossed? Do we need to put a boundary in place?

DISPELLING NEGATIVE EMOTIONS AND ACCESSING THE INFORMATION THEY HAVE FOR US

Uncomfortable and painful emotions have been deemed negative by our culture and, in turn, have gotten a bad rap. When we avoid a label or categorizing negative and positive, we can sit with the emotion. *We have been taught that negative emotions are bad and positive emotions are good. What if we throw all the labels away?* When we resist the emotion, which can be a common reaction with so-called negative emotions, they don't typically disappear. My observations have shown me that this is when people can feel overwhelmed by their emotions—powerless to them, which can lead to fits of rage or isolation, along with many other unconscious reactions. Rather, when we turn toward the emotion and consciously choose to have it and sit with it, we can access the information it has for us. While the emotion may come with some discomfort, how uncomfortable is the avoidance or fear it causes? Let's look at this in a real-world scenario.

I have a client whose mother is undiagnosed but likely on the autism spectrum. My client did not discover this until he was in his midforties. His mother is also a narcissist. This has caused him pain throughout his life, but because of her condition, there was no way to resolve this pain with her. Moreover, when he tried to have conversations with her, they became all about her, and there wasn't room for his experience.

Consequently, my client bottled up his emotions to placate the situation. He swallowed his hurt and his anger, again and again. This began to result in his anger seeping into other areas of his life. He might snap at his kids, or scream at a car that cut him off, or start to get short with teammates, impacting his standing at work. Swallowing his emotions was not actually doing the trick. Rather, it was delaying his experience of them until it came out in unintentional ways.

So we made space for the anger. When he had an interaction with his mother that left him feeling hurt or angry, he had a couple of people he could call and set a time limit (maybe five or ten minutes) to express his frustration, pain, and rage. This was not to fix anything or work through anything but just to experience the emotion and then move through it. In doing this, he was able to *have* his emotion rather than *being had* by it. By engaging his anger with curiosity, he learned a lot about what he cared about, the truth he wasn't communicating, and what he may have been protecting or scared to lose. Discomfort is a great door opener to new information, new ways of being, and even the newest version of ourselves. "Okay enough" can be a tricky place to negotiate.

Discomfort can also be a great motivator to get unstuck, as long as we investigate it. *"Okay enough" can keep us stuck.*

Discomfort often also falls into the negative category. What has come from discomfort in your life? Was it the beginning or cause of change? Of new growth? When we look at the role of discomfort in our lives, we can begin to see its value. Perhaps it encouraged a move, leaving a relationship, shifting careers, or breaking or starting a new habit.

I often wonder if it was a disservice to put "the pursuit of happiness" in our nation's Declaration of Independence. It did two things. First, it took happiness outside ourselves and put it someplace—out there—to go and get. Second, it certainly put a stigma on the emotions deemed as negative: fear, grief, sadness, anger, and so on—and these emotions are so rich. They have much information for us and are often the home of our growth if we'll only examine them more closely. For the more challenging elements, there's a mindset I apply that I find to be very helpful—and I'm not implying it's always easy; it can be very challenging. Rather than viewing things as why they are happening *to* me, I view them through the lens of why they are happening *for* me.

Sometimes it feels like the hardest time to practice curiosity—such as when life has put you in a circumstance where it can feel easy to be the victim. You get a flat tire. You get laid off. You get sick. It's easy to add to the weight of the burden by leaning into the victim mindset. What if curiosity plays a role?

What if getting a flat tire put you off the road to avoid a traffic accident you may have been in?

What if getting laid off led you to the perfect next job you wouldn't have been looking for if you were satisfied enough in your existing circumstance?

What if getting sick helped you slow down and give your body some much needed rest, which contributes to your larger sense of well-being? Stress is dis-ease that can lead to disease. Remember, we fear because what we value, what's most important to us, is being threatened. In essence, then, our fear can serve as our research and development department for mining for our values and intentional living as long as we take the time to learn what fear is showing us. Once we recognize fear is here, we can begin to practice to turn toward it rather than run away from it or avoid it, in order to see what information fear has for us.

MAKING ROOM FOR FEAR

Engaging with fear may feel uncomfortable at first. When we work out a new muscle group, it can hurt and become sore. The shift from fear into courage (or simply choice) may cause a little discomfort. Typically change doesn't come from a place of comfort. Our growth takes place outside our comfort zone. If we write the story that fear is a teacher and not the enemy, we can create a safe way to explore the information it has for us. Curiosity enables you to be the active participant instead of the narrator.

> ## PRACTICE
> What is your fear trying to tell you? Allow yourself to acknowledge the fear. When you notice yourself in fear (running a what-if storyline), pause. Ask yourself,
> - What do I know is true?
> - What am I telling myself is true?
> - What am I curious about? Where do I need more information?
> - What is it that matters the most to me at this moment?

Once we make room for our fear, even welcome it, then we begin to be in conversation with it. What if when we felt our fear, instead of turning away from it, we stared right at it, asked, "What are you here to show me?" and engaged it in a conversation. It's a little uncomfortable at first, but the more we understand the process, the less uncomfortable it becomes. Your fear knows more about you than anyone. It knows what you really want (what you're scared of), what you desire (where you want to grow), and what steps you need to take to get there (the very place where you may feel like an imposter). If we grow curious about fear's language, there's rich meaning to be had for our own self-discovery.

When we're in unhealthy fear, we are in an assumption. We are running a what-if, future-tense scenario. We are telling ourselves a story that may not be grounded in facts or reflective of our current reality. Further, our curiosity is not present when we are writing a story. We can't be simultaneously curious and making assumptions—just as we can't at the same time be in fear and curiosity.

What is the language of your fear? What are the stories you're telling yourself? What are its messages? How does it narrate the story of your day? Fear may sound different for you than it does for a friend of yours. Whenever a client tells me they have a fear or they feel the imposter syndrome, I ask them to share with me the language their fear is using. What exact verbiage and stories is fear telling you? That's important information to help us decode the truth.

If we're telling ourselves stories, we may as well tell ourselves stories that benefit us.

THE CONSTRUCT OF TIME

One story that comes up with most of my clients is the story of time. "There is never enough time to get to all the things I have to get to," they say. Most people start their days with this story.

A client of mine was a chief learning officer of a public company on the road to an IPO (a full-time job in itself), and she was writing a book and preparing for a TED Talk. Time was limited. However, whenever we connected, the emphasis was on the lack of time. Not everything could get done in the time allotted; there just wasn't enough time; the lack of time is a burden. These stories take us out of the present moment and feed a loop of worry that makes everything harder. Only a part of us is actually working in that moment, if we're more worried about what won't get done.

My client began to practice a mantra that stated she had the time she needed to get to everything on her to-do list. Did it stretch time? Or did it just appear to? It enabled her to take deep breaths—another thing we don't tend to do when we're running anxious stories of not having enough time—and allowed her to work on the most important thing that had to be done next. All of that contributed to better sleep—a key element during such a busy time.

Our brains aren't invested in what's best for us. They're like data centers that are trying to validate whatever data we're giving it. So, if we're feeding it the truth that there's not enough time in the day to get to everything we need to, our brain is going to validate that truth with all the data it can—because we are reinforcing that belief by claiming it. Moreover, most of us are running our minds and bodies on this loop from the time we awaken.

Time is a funny construct. An hour doesn't always feel like an hour. It depends on what you're doing. Are you enjoying the task or moment? Are you present in that moment? Are you carrying the burden of not having enough time? Are you future thinking or past-time shaming? I give a simple mantra to many clients who are struggling with this plight—and watch them move into more spaciousness.

Instead of ruminating on how much there is to do and how there's not enough time, try opening to a more supportive relationship with time. By getting curious and opening to how you might experience time differently, you can create a story that will serve you.

Whether you're in the shower, getting dressed, or closing your morning meditation, claim the following: *There is more than enough time in the day to get to all the things I need to with additional space* (or something similar that resonates). See if it brings about shifts. Does it feel like time slows down? Maybe you have time to get to that workout class you didn't think you could fit in. Maybe the project you were working on only took two hours instead of the days you thought it might. Maybe you had time to play with your child when you thought you'd be working late. Repeat this mantra as needed throughout the day, especially if you hear yourself running a lack-of-time storyline.

SEEDS TO PLANT

- What-if future thinking comprises stories we create.
- Curiosity can help us access the present moment and our truth.
- We fear because something we value may be threatened.
- Masks of fear distract us from having to face the underlying fear they're protecting.
- What information can we access when we throw away the positive and negative labels of emotions–and see them as information?
- "Okay enough" is the home of stuck.
- New framing: *Why is this happening for me* versus *Why is this happening to me?*
- If we're telling ourselves stories, we may as well tell ourselves stories that serve us and cast us in the roles we want to play.

CHAPTER 8

THE POWER OF GRATITUDE

Gratitude bestows reverence, changing forever how we experience life and the world.
—John Milton

I'm not religious. If it needed to be defined, I'd call myself spiritual, but I do have a religion. It's gratitude. To me, gratitude is a direct line to the Universe giving thanks for what I want to receive. *It's a tangible way to practice awe rather than waiting for those rare glimpses of it.* The more gratitude I have, the more I'm graced with things to be grateful for.

This applies to all things, those perceived as negative and positive. It's easy to practice gratitude with pleasurable elements. More challenging situations can be harder to connect to gratitude—maybe an unexpected job loss or a realization you may have hurt a friend, even if unintentionally, and need to address it. This is really where I get the opportunity to practice why this is happening *for* me versus why this is happening *to* me, because this mindset is one that supports my growth and my healing. Maybe the loss of that job has me looking for a new one when I otherwise wouldn't be—and that job is more in line with what I actually want to do, or in a work culture that's more conducive to collaboration. In the case of the realization with the friend, hard conversations can be challenging. So can owning what we can do differently. Leaning into that honest conversation might even bring more depth to the connection going forward.

GRATITUDE IS A FRAMING FOR CHOOSING TO VIEW EXPERIENCES

A lot of times, the greatest fears we face are rooted in scarcity. We don't have enough time, talent, skill sets—because we don't have enough. The underlying belief here is "I'm not enough." Fear has us focus on the lack, thereby creating a perpetual cycle of a mindset of lack.

Glenn Fox, head of University of Southern California Performance Science Institute, conducted a study, "Neural Correlates of Gratitude," published in the academic journal *Frontiers in Psychology*, that found that when participants reported grateful feelings, their brains showed activity in the prefrontal cortex, the home of curiosity, expression, decision-making, and connection. Gratitude, like curiosity, is a quality that can move us from our amygdala to our prefrontal cortex, neurologically shifting us out of fear. This may feel counterintuitive, as for most of us, it may feel foreign to practice gratitude when we're experiencing fear.

In every aspect of life—from personal relationships to leading businesses—cultivating gratitude for the assets we have, and the opportunities challenges may present, will help us be more creative with those assets and circumstances. This can be a multitude of things:

the depth of a relationship, the joy it brings you, the growth it asks of you, the call you can make when you need a friend, the beauty of nature and its ability to bring calm to us, the team that takes the risks and fails and is stronger for it, the vulnerability you expressed as a leader to call forth your team's best, the deep grief after losing someone (connecting you to the love you have for them). Some of these might be harder than others. We can find gratitude in every circumstance if we look for it. It's a way of framing our experience —and it's a choice.

I realize it may seem a big leap to be grateful for your fear but hear me out. Why am I a defender of fear? Fear is the key to our freedom. If they are left unexplored, we give our power away to our fears. If we take our power back and use it to mine the information our fears have for us, we learn who we really are and are shown the steps we need to take to get there, to grow into the next version of ourselves. *Nothing has more information for us than our fears.* Even if it has an ironic sense of humor (making us dread the very thing we desire), fear is the only language fear speaks. Expecting my fear to speak Guryan to me would be like me thinking that if I speak in English to a speaker of Mandarin, they could understand what I was saying. If they learned English, they could understand what I had said. If I learn the language of fear, perhaps I can understand what my fears are saying. What an invitation for us to get curious about the language of our fears—so that we can access the gifts of personal wisdom fear has for each of us.

Being grateful for our fears helps us see them as our allies instead of our enemies. Most of us are aware of what fear has prevented us from doing, what we regret not doing, what we've missed out on, what it has cost us. On the flip side, have you ever wondered how your fears have served you? What have they caused you to do or not to do? Our fear has contributed to shaping who we are, and when we understand how it's in service to us, we can be grateful for the role it plays in connecting us to our most authentic self.

I'll share a very high-level example with you. I have undiagnosed OCD tendencies. When I'm looking at them through a mindset of lack or fear—which means when I'm judging or shaming myself about these tendencies—I have a fear of being perceived as high-maintenance and intractable. When I look at my OCD through a how-is-this-serving-me? mindset, which can connect me to the gifts these tendencies have for me, I have an incredible level of efficiency, which often enables me to accomplish things at a superpower level. Those who know me are aware of my love for to-do lists. They're not for everyone, but they help bring structure to set up my efficiency for success. Let's say I have a trip I'm planning or packing for, errands that have to be run to prepare for it, a slide deck that needs to be made for a presentation I'm giving, and people to see before I head out. Even if the feeling of overwhelm creeps in, I pause, use my I-have-enough-time mantra, and then lean into my OCD and watch things get done at a rate that surprises even me.

Often we are familiar with what challenges come with negatively perceived emotions, like anxiety, but we don't acknowledge the gifts they may have for us. Many clients come to me stating they have high levels of anxiety. I am not taking away from the (in some cases, grave) challenges that anxiety presents. I also believe it's worth looking at how anxiety may serve us. Some of the common traits in my clients with high anxiety levels are that they are detail oriented, compassionate, thoughtful, highly curious. . . . I could go on. When we can identify all the attributes that are available to us when we're in different states (fear, anger, anxiety), we have more choices for dialing up or down and when.

To walk you through this, let me return to my example of my OCD tendencies. If I'm home alone, I can dial them up as I'm the only one they're impacting. If, however, I am with a group of people, perhaps I consider the impact they may have and choose to dial them down. I can shift into engaging these tendencies intentionally rather than being held hostage by them. For example, in my refrigerator, things may be organized from shortest to tallest from front to back (so I can see exactly what's in there). But when I'm at a friend's place, I'll let them choose how to, or not to, organize their fridge. I won't mention a thing. My idiosyncrasies might work for me and seem absurd to another.

We tend to focus on what fear has prevented us from. What if we consider these other perspectives? In the practice of gratitude, I invite you to connect with a perceived negative attribute of one of your fears to identify how it has served you. For example, I selected my OCD tendencies. What's one for you? Are you hesitant? Intense? Anxious? Soft-spoken? You are likely well aware of all that it has cost you—all that has probably been on a loop in your mental story creation department. What if you also acknowledged how your fear has served you?

I know this can be tricky at first. If you're looking at something like anxiety, for example, the gifts may include things like thoughtfulness, attention to detail, compassion, awareness, patience, and so on. How has this attribute, which you may have only before associated with negative connotations, also been a positive for you?

> **PRACTICE**
>
> What attribute do you feel insecure about? What perception are you afraid of?
>
> Now let's move to what gifts your insecurity has had for you.
>
> Take a moment to write a thank-you note to this attribute.
>
> Thank you _____ [fill in perceived negative attribute] for. . . .
>
> What has this fear helped you achieve?
>
> How has this fear served you personally?

GRATITUDE CONNECTS US TO WHAT WE WANT

Being grateful for our fears gives us access to our one-of-a-kind puzzle pieces. Gratitude can also connect us to what we value most. Our fears have helped make us who we are today. *When we begin to connect with our gratitude, we can create a safe container for beginning to engage our fear in a different way.* Let me share another example, one where more was at stake.

Those who knew me in my younger years may recall sharing a cigarette or two with me on the outside deck of one of the companies we worked at together, or curbside during the evening bar rendezvous. I started smoking when I was fourteen, and I will say that I was—as with most things I do—committed to it (and I loved it). Over time, as smoking became less socially acceptable, the only thing I was committed to more than smoking was hiding it from others. In 2011, one of the great gifts my ex-husband gave me was helping me move to the e-cigarette (as, at the time, we thought it was a much healthier option). For eight years, I had been using this alternative. The irony is that I probably ended up smoking more because it's incredibly easy to hide, you don't have to go outside, and there's no life to it (a cigarette burns out, where an e-cigarette goes on forever —as long as you let it, that is). Here's a record of the eleven days in 2019 when I stopped using nicotine:

Monday, September 16, 2019: I awoke to the headline that nine people had died from unexplained respiratory illness linked to e-cigarettes.

Tuesday, September 17: I awoke to chest pain. I told myself if I can swim the mile I do every morning, I'm fine (trying to continue the denial I'd practiced for twenty-five years). I swam the mile. My chest pain remained. I continued to smoke.

Wednesday, September 18: I applied the same mental and physical morning test. If I can swim my mile, I'm fine. I swam the mile. I cleared my afternoon to get into nature. The chest pain remained. I continued to smoke.

Thursday, September 19: I applied the same mental and physical morning test. If I can swim my mile, I'm fine. I swam the mile. By midday, I became lightheaded and thought I might pass out. The fear was loud. I cleared my afternoon and drove myself to the ER. The chest pain remained. I continued to smoke on my drive there. After receiving the most amazing bill of health possible (chest X-rays, EKG, blood oxygen test), I drove home. I continued to smoke.

Five days pass . . . same drill.

Tuesday, September 24: I awoke to the newest related headline. The count was now up to twelve unexplained deaths linked to e-cigarettes. As I grasped onto denial as hard as I could, the mental unraveling began.

Wednesday, September 25: My first day in twenty-five years without a cigarette.

Quitting smoking was the hardest thing I've ever had to do. At my lowest point, I took a walk, and for each step I took, I said the name out loud of someone in my life whom I cared for deeply, for whom I wouldn't take my own life, someone I was grateful to walk this life with. It was *that hard*—physically, emotionally, mentally, and energetically. Each element had its own experience. Withdrawals, sadness, and the releasing of emotion that I had probably been swallowing for twenty-five years; shame, recognition of my strength or courage (sadly, this was least present in the first couple weeks); restriction, expansion, suppression, pissed-off-ed-ness; repatterning of neural pathways, distraction, and and and . . .

I knew cigarettes kill. We all know that. My denial was louder than my knowledge—until my inner truth was even louder. Smoking is not who I am. It's not in integrity with what I stand for—and talk about a hardening agent when I've been enabling my own softening for years. In this case, fear saved me. I think my higher self knew the only way to get me to stop smoking was to scare the shit out of me, so it found the intersection of rational and irrational fear and rescued me. It connected me to my truth: *This is not who I am.*

It did take courage. Thank goodness my fear was showing me where to apply it.

Exploring our fears grants us access to greater truths.

When we connect to what we're grateful for, we can increase our intentionality of bringing more into our lives of what we actually want to attract. *Where we put our energy grows.* If there's something in my life I want to invite in to attract, I bring my energy to that intention and I express my gratitude for it—which often builds upon what I already have. And if I am experiencing lack, I use that as an opportunity to connect to what is important about what it is I feel lack around, so it can become something I consciously invite in and become aware of that so that I can shift patterns (old protective mechanisms) that may be blocking its emergence. And what if we are putting our energy toward that which we want to reduce? It can be common to let fearful stories run. One of my clients called it, "What-if-ism." Where we put our attention grows. If we're running our energy around what we want less of, we will attract that too.

PRACTICE

Take a mason jar or big glass jar (make sure it's clear so that over time you can see the gratitudes grow).

Get a stack of Post-it notes.

Every morning when you wake up, write down one thing you are grateful for.

Repeat through the day and evening.

Gratitude for something doesn't always mean it's fun or even enjoyable. Just finding gratitude for the challenge is often what's being asked of us. Growing pains can ask us to stretch.

We can start small. When I found myself at the bottom of that rabbit hole, the simplest appreciations helped orient me to my center and could

The fastest way to shift from scarcity to abundance is gratitude.

be for my able body (to exercise or walk with), my breath (to bring me ease and connect me to my center), a person who reached out to share a connection with me (to share a walk, a conversation, a hug), the capacity of my heart (as it's growing and grieving), and so on.

SEEDS TO PLANT

- Gratitude is a tangible way to practice awe.
- Like curiosity, gratitude can neurologically move us from our fear center (amygdala) to our prefrontal cortex.
- Fear is the only language fear speaks, making it worthwhile for us to learn its language.
- Practicing gratitude creates a safe container to explore fear differently.
- Where we put our energy grows.
- Is what-if-ism present? Be mindful of its contagious power.
- The fastest way to shift from scarcity to abundance is gratitude.
- How have your fears served you? What can you genuinely thank them for?

CHAPTER 9

THE ROLE OF PURPOSE

> *The privilege of a lifetime*
> *is being who you truly are.*
> —Joseph Campbell

What if we could shift unintentional reactions to intentional responses? The freedom to escape from boxed-in thinking and systems that aren't serving us rises to the top and helps us live in choice versus shoulds. "Should" and "conform" go hand in hand, so notice when you "should" yourself and are not living in the freedom to be your authentic self and express your truth—in other words, to live on purpose. Instead, we must begin to free ourselves by using the very fears that hold us back and, in so doing, create genuine community and connection through purpose.

AUTHENTICITY SERVES A PURPOSE

Living on purpose is a way to be our authentic self, which is our greatest freedom. Remember those eight billion fingerprints? From such young ages we're taught to conform. This is what success looks like (we're sold). This is what beauty looks like (we're shown). This is what happiness includes (we're told). What boxes can we put ourselves in to more easily navigate a system of even more boxes? It's never ending. However, what if our fingerprints are the reminder that signifies to us that we're all here to make our own impression? By embracing our uniqueness and being our authentic self, we can be seen, and from this place we can see others for their uniqueness. *The ability to embrace our own uniqueness takes the power away from feeling the need to conform.* What's your impression to make? And how can you be impacted by witnessing others' unique impression?

Fear reveals our deepest values through our personal expression, contentment, family, and participation in some purpose that's bigger than ourselves. Fear is bringing our attention to something about which we care deeply. We could be scared of everything—but we're not. By mining our fears, we can remove the obstacle—fear's way of trying to keep us safe—that prevents us from connecting to our purpose: what's most important, what we're in service of, and who we truly are.

One of the fascinating things I've found in all my years of coaching is that when I ask people what their values are, many haven't taken the time to understand them or connect with them. Of course they/we haven't. Values haven't been made a priority and aren't part of the constructs that run our current systems. However, we value what is most important to us. When we get triggered by a partner, stranger, colleague, or boss, it's often because something important to us is being threatened. Maybe our values aren't being honored. But if we don't know what they are, how can we behave in a way that brings them into being? Moreover, how can we respond thoughtfully and intentionally instead of relying on the unhealthy reactions of fight, flight, freeze, or fawn (rage, isolation, paralysis, and appeasement)? Learning about our values is an eye-opening journey, so let's take a moment.

PRACTICE

Get a piece of paper and a pen.

Begin by writing down your values. All of them. You may have eight, you may have eighty.

By way of example: equanimity, curiosity, social justice, integrity, compassion, creative expression, community, and so on.

Once you've exhausted your list, circle the five that are most alive for you at this moment. As you change and grow over time, your values may evolve over time. We're a constantly evolving life force influenced by our environments and relationships and experiences.

Next it's time to discover what your values mean to you. It's time to—as I refer to this part of the process—"go into them," or explore them in greater detail. Two people may have different interpretations for the same value, such as integrity, so it's important to clarify as much as possible your personal take on the value. First, connect to what it means to you. Write down your definition of the value. Then connect to why that's important to you. Write this down beneath the definition. Put it somewhere you can see it. Familiarize yourself with what matters most to you.

Here is an example of one of my client's values maps:

Value—Oneness: *Feeling connected with everyone else, everything else—that we're one living organism. There is togetherness and harmony. This is unity.*

> **Why:** *It's the opposite of loneliness. How we're connected with the larger group. Togetherness makes me feel hopeful.*

Value—Growth: *Never giving up on your own (and other's) potential. Believing in your and their full potential to realize themselves (seeing beyond what currently is and making it happen).*

> **Why:** *It gives me hope. No matter how hard life is— there's a chance for betterment (for self and others).*

Value—Hope: *The thing that keeps you going when everything else is hard. What unlocks new possibilities for you—and others.*

> **Why:** *What drives my perseverance. It makes things dynamic. It makes water flow.*

Value—Love: *Not only loving others—but loving yourself. Self-compassion. Not needing a justification. Just caring and seeing the beauty in who I am/they are. Kindness and being gentle. It's forgiveness.*

> **Why:** *It's not just about someone's accomplishments—it's the beingness of a person.*

Value—Spirit: *Something bigger than the physical world. Faith. Belief in something larger.*

> **Why**: *Some of the best moments I had in my life are related to spirituality.*

Values can serve as the framework to help you walk your talk. Like anything, living by your values is a practice. When you speak to someone who meditates, rarely do they say, "I meditated once."

They often tell you they meditate daily. Practicing our values is just that. A practice. We have had a lot of practice at letting our self-critic take the lead as well as our doubts, anger, and insecurities. *What if we begin to practice what it is that we want more of as opposed to that which is depleting us?*

As I mentioned, I found myself in open space after leaving my marriage and my job. I learned something about the power of liminality at that time. When we walk away from something (a marriage, job, home, city, friendship), we also walk away from a previous version of ourselves. Before the newest version of ourselves emerges, we find ourselves in a space between: the liminal. Between who we were and who we're becoming is one of the richest places of our existence—and can be uncomfortable when we're unaware of this stage of the process of transition.

In that space, all that I hadn't looked at—some conscious and some subconscious—was waiting for me, staring me in the eyes, relentlessly asking for my attention. It was around this time I turned more intentionally to meditation. I had a practice of meditation before. However, in order to be in the space, I needed a foundation for beginning my days and my exploration. Sometimes presence came gently to me, and at other times I struggled with its elusiveness. The longer I sat, the harder it got to be with the space, because as I sat there, I discovered something was missing: purpose. I felt plagued with purpose, only I didn't know what my purpose was—but I discovered something about the pit in my stomach.

We rarely find ourselves in a liminal space. It's so rich with potential and tenderness and presence—in part because our minds can't write a story yet. There isn't enough fodder. When I find myself in these moments or am coaching someone through this time, my favorite framing is to invite myself and others to notice how we are showing up differently. For example, are you saying no to things you would before have automatically said yes to? Are you caring less about someone else's opinion of you? Are you interested in something new that hadn't been on your radar? Observe this newest you that is unfolding. The only story I have found to support these times is: *Who am I? I don't know. . . . I'm just meeting her.*

PURPOSE GIVES US DIRECTION

Purpose is a big concept. Sometimes conversations around purpose can feel a little ethereal, vague, or academic, but nothing could be further from the truth. Purpose shows up in a million real-world decisions that impact our lives and the lives around us. This could be your dedication to building a community—or being a part of one. It might be being a master gardener. Perhaps being the most present father. It could be a life committed to a cause that you care about (education, climate, breaking down divisions, etc.). It could be the commitment to live your values. As individuals, when we're in touch with our authentic purpose, our choices become more intentional and lead to more contentment and freedom. For example, when you know community is your purpose, then the choices you make can support what's best for the community, what brings you closer, what expands your community further, and so on.

Purpose doesn't have to be audacious. It's not about being Nelson Mandela, Steve Jobs, or Serena Williams, as a few examples. Purpose is about being who we truly are. *Rather than accomplishing a life's purpose, what if we live on purpose?* If we have a life purpose and accomplish it, what do we do then? It's not a box to check or something to accomplish, it's a way of being. Living on purpose is when we have purpose at the center of our awareness and the choices we make support it. That present father? Maybe he has a business trip in New York City but decides to fly home to Austin on Friday night so that he can be there when his kids wake up on Saturday rather than extending the trip for a night out in the city. Purpose allows for intentional living. When I'm acting in service to purpose, it becomes a navigational guide. Our purpose is our values in action, serving as a North Star, giving us guidance on our path, and helping us reorient if we lose that path. This is how we practice accountability. How do our choices line up with what we say is most important to us?

Purpose can help keep us in integrity.

Additionally, purpose is a practice of hope, which I believe is the future tense of love. We were never told that grief is love. I believe it is. We are grieving the loss of something we cared for, something we loved. It's the absence of something that no longer is there—and thus becomes past tense. Hope is what we're longing into being. It's what we intend, what we desire, what we want to make manifest. Hope can be a gateway to reframing—which can create the mindset that runs the narrative of our reality. With a purpose we can set our intentions to ensure we're choosing to live our life intentionally, in service of what makes us most alive—and the world we're wanting to make possible. Most people fear the unknowns. When we think of the future, it's possible to run hundreds of what-if scenarios that may play out scary storylines that we are living in volatile times. Hope helps give us a framing of what we want to bring into being—enabling us to be an active participant in creating our future rather than allowing storylines of fear to prevail.

The Role of Purpose

If purpose is our North Star, hope can give a sense of reorientation as we navigate challenging times. In fact, in many different instances (some juvenile delinquent centers, the Holocaust, some medical institutions, autoimmune disorders), the absence of hope has been described as lethal—a very interesting word. What if we didn't underestimate the power of hope? Of a future-tense-abundant mindset as opposed to a future-state what-if mindset of lack that leaves our fear unexplored to keep us where we are.

We find ourselves now in times when hope isn't just nice to have; it's imperative. I'm reminded of Howard Zinn's words in *You Can't Be Neutral on a Moving Train:*

> To be hopeful in bad times is not just foolishly romantic. It is based on the fact that human history is a history not only of cruelty, but also of compassion, sacrifice, courage, kindness. What we choose to emphasize in this complex history will determine our lives. If we see only the worst, it destroys our capacity to do something. If we remember those times and

places—and there are so many—where people have behaved magnificently, this gives us the energy to act, and at least the possibility of sending this spinning top of a world in a different direction. And if we do act, in however small a way, we don't have to wait for some grand utopian future. The future is an infinite succession of presents, and to live now as we think human beings should live, in defiance of all that is bad around us, is itself a marvelous victory.

We create the future path. It's not being bestowed upon us. *What is possible when purpose is at the core of our behaviors, choices, and society?* This process is about moving into choice—intentional responses instead of unintentional reactions. And what do intentional responses begin with? An intention. It all comes down to choice. When we're in fear, we give our power away and then we are no longer able to make rational choices. What does it mean to be intentional about our choices?

One of the gifts of having purpose is it becomes a tool to quiet the fears while we work to befriend them. This leads me to a helpful mantra I use...

If I have something I'm in service to, my discomfort is not as grave because what I'm in service to is more important than my discomfort. A client and friend is in service to peace, which for her means going around the country to do walks for peace. She sits with people as their lives end to support them with an energy of peace as they make their final end-of-life transition. It means she wants to engage in conversation with those who think differently than her to understand their perspective, to learn more about their experience, to see

My why is bigger than I.

if there is common ground. These are hard situations that can bring plenty of discomfort, but her commitment to peace supersedes her discomfort. She might question herself how can she, as one person, create peace? However, her why (being in service to peace) is bigger than her doubt about what she as one person can do. Purpose doesn't have to be your life purpose; it can be the purpose for a particular interaction or act of service. For example, do you build in a few extra minutes when you go to your community center to see how Heidi, the eighty-six-year-old woman you know who doesn't have anyone at home to talk to, is doing? When I live my purpose, I feel my most alive. Whenever we're engaged with anything, there can be a why to it, a purpose to it—a "What are you in service of?"

For me, as I have mentioned, my why is how to create a world of and not or. This takes on many faces: finding common ground, seeking understanding, experiencing many feelings and sensations at once. Every time I have a decision to make, I can choose to see it through this lens. How can I make a choice that stays true to my guiding light, the thing that drives me the most? My intention is and not or, which gives me the opportunity to find my true resonance in every circumstance I find myself in, even if it's hard, especially when it's hard. Even if it means listening to someone I disagree with.

My relationship with my dad has been challenging. It is, after all, the core of my basal fear, the fear of abandonment. We did the estranged thing for over two decades. It was incredibly hard. We have found a way to come back together and the hard still remains, though now it's a different hard. There are remnants from what we went through—and I am also hurt by recent actions and decisions he makes. It's important for me to have a relationship with him because he is my father and I love him, even if it isn't always the relationship

I wanted—and want—it to be. This allows us both to have our experience and for me to be truthful to my needs instead of rejecting him for the fear of being hurt. Because I'm able to be intentional about his presence in my life and how I want to show up, the pain isn't all encompassing. Sometimes it walks beside me, and I can hold its hand. Having him in my life (and) is more important than not having him in it at all (or). How am I practicing living truthfully to my strongest intention? It's how I practice my values. How do I live my intention so that I can make an intentional choice? It's a practice I must choose, again and again and again.

I want to underscore the importance of intentionality. We can set an intention for every interaction we're going to have (personal and professional) about the way we want to show up, the way we want to listen, the way we want to connect from our hearts with others. So in the moment, we're able to make an intentional choice by remembering how we said we wanted to show up—and checking to see if we're staying true to that.

The reason I decided to lean into "and" was the expansiveness it gives you to get curious, to explore, to adapt. The power of "and" is immense. "And" is a doorway out of binary thinking, a movement away from right and wrong. It creates space enabling us to learn about new perspectives for ourselves or even those offered to us by someone we're engaging. "And" is full of possibilities. It enables openness and curiosity, and it can break down division. In addition to being my North Star, "and" also serves as a tool for building conversation as opposed to shutting it down. This decreases division and expands space for more (thought, idea, connection, etc.) to exist within. When listening to someone whom we may not agree with, rather than focusing on what we disagree on, there's an opportunity to create a bridge-building dialogue.

A hard line is often in place when someone has a fear, when something they care deeply about is being threatened. When we understand our own relationship with fear, we can begin to see when others may be acting from a place of fear—without being aware of it. What if the focus was on what they were protecting? What are they afraid of losing? What is important to them? It doesn't mean this will bring agreement. Resolution might be the coexistence of important things for different people. However, it doesn't shut someone down and potentially stoke the fears further.

In addition to listening to someone I may not currently agree with, being in service of my "and" (committed to the practice of openness, exploration, and multi-experiential living), there are a number of ways this opportunity can present itself to practice—perhaps when two circumstances seem opposing.

Let me give you an example. Years ago, I hadn't heard from a girlfriend in some time. At that time, my husband and I had been going through fertility treatments (which were long-lasting and unsuccessful—but that's another story). After a long length of time with no communication, she showed up at my apartment, pregnant and in tears. I inquired what was wrong. Was she okay? Was the baby okay? She shared with me that she was scared to tell me she was pregnant because of the challenges my then husband and I were going through. I looked at her and assured her—we could cry for me and celebrate for her in the same visit. What I was more scared of was losing the closeness between us because our paths may have been going through different twists and turns.

In this case, while the circumstances we were both navigating appeared like opposites, I wasn't against her becoming pregnant because I was having difficulty. Further, it allowed me to feel multiple emotions at once. Very rarely do we just experience one emotion in isolation; moreover, sometimes they can feel contrary. For example, when experiencing loss of a person, we may feel the pain of letting go as well as the joy of having known the person. We might be experiencing intense grief and hope simultaneously. The "and" allows us to dance among them, and anything else we're feeling, from moment to moment, all in service to the purpose that is guiding us.

PUTTING PURPOSE INTO PRACTICE

Identifying our North Star may feel like an audacious, time-consuming, or even daunting undertaking, and the payoff may not be immediately obvious. When we look deeper at the fears that hold us back from examining our purpose, they shed light on why it's such an important exercise. What's more, exploring our fear courageously is an incredibly effective way to reconnect with our purpose on a deeper level. Whatever it is, fear points us toward what matters most, what we're in service of—who we are—our purpose. Fear can be our flashlight, illuminating the path to purpose for our courage to walk on.

Finding purpose begins with the first gateway: curiosity. And the initial area of focus is a place many feel uncomfortable with: ourselves. Curiosity leads to rewarding and sometimes difficult questions.

> **REFLECTION**
>
> Ask yourself some substantive questions:
>
> What am I doing when I feel most alive?
>
> What is most important for me to protect?
>
> What kind of future am I trying to create—or contribute to?
>
> What is my true expression? What do I love to do?
>
> What sparks my curiosity with valor?
>
> Do I feel connected to my purpose?
>
> What is preventing me from realizing my purpose?
>
> How does my purpose align with my own belief system?
>
> How am I practicing it in my daily life?
>
> How could I be served by being more intentional about seeing through the lens of my purpose as I navigate my days?
>
> What is the unique contribution I want to make to my family, community, a stranger, the world, or whatever you connect with most?
>
> You may not have all the answers at once. Start with what you do know. Sit in inquiry with what you're wanting to connect with more deeply. It's a process.

When we live on purpose (guided by our why), we open ourselves to new input and ways of thinking, from which we can contribute our unique perspective and create from a place of connection. What's possible with our why? Community. Regeneration. Collective empowerment. What does your why make possible for you?

We can take what means the most to us, understand why it matters, and connect to what's possible if we put it into action. If you find such connection challenging, here's a visualization that may help you discover your *why*.

PRACTICE

Close your eyes.

Pick your favorite car (if you don't drive, then select the ideal car to be in for a drive). What color is it? Are the windows down? Convertible top down?

Now choose your favorite landscape (snowy mountains, coastal cliffs, farmland, tropics—anything that makes your heart feel calm).

Go for your drive/ride. . . Take in your surroundings. The visuals. The smells. The sounds.

Up ahead in the distance there are three billboards.

As you get closer, you see they're blank. They're yours. You can share three messages with the world. These are the three things you care the most about.

What would you tell people? What would you wish everyone knew is possible? What would you want people to know as they navigate this life?

Write down your three messages:

Billboard 1: _____

Billboard 2: _____

Billboard 3: _____

These have important messages for you. They are connecting you to what you stand for. These messages often represent ways of being versus accomplishments and outcomes, painting pictures of what's possible when we act in service of purpose and our authentic selves. If our purpose is being who we truly are, then knowing what we stand for, what matters the most to us, can help us connect to who we are.

How can you implement this in your daily life? When faced with a decision, the practice can be used in two ways. First, see whatever decision or circumstance you're facing through the lens of your *why*. Be intentional about which of your key values you'd like to exemplify in your behaviors when you make decisions. Can it become a choice? With practice, it can—even when it's hard.

Let's look at the role that "and" can play when we're experiencing some of the more challenging elements like loss, grief, and letting go. Many of us experience loss in varying forms again and again throughout our lives. This could be the loss of a job, someone you love (a relationship ending or by death), a milestone accomplished (graduation, completion of a project), and so on. What if there's a way to let go and have hope—to let go of what was and grieving that in whatever ways feel nourishing to you and holding out hope for more of what it brought you. That could be more connection, more ideation, more inspiration, and so forth. Both loss and hope exist. And both are worthy of our energy. And another opportunity for gratitude. Can we also be thankful for the experience? Imagine how your life would have suffered without it.

Once you've connected to your why, get curious about the world it makes possible. With the father who returned early from his New York business trip's case, what does that mean for his child? For the community builder, what will people benefit from? Deep connection? Events? Volunteer opportunities? For the peace walker, a slightly less divided world? How do people sense your why? Does it make you feel alive? Impassioned? Present? How does it impact the way you show up to the moments in your life? When put at the forefront of our decision-making, purpose can serve as our unwavering constant guiding light. It's a tool for connecting to the present moment, and once we are present, it is possible to be in choice at every moment.

He who has a why to live for can endure any how.
—Friedrich Nietzsche

What's the cost if we don't align to our why? If there ever was a time to orient around a guiding purpose, it's the moment we are living through right now. Climate change, artificial intelligence, racial injustice, financial instability, generational shifts, and political divisiveness have generated rising levels of uncertainty, concern leading to panic, and decisions made from a standpoint of fear. This is the scenario in which we risk losing our authentic path forward. When we practice unhealthy fear—consciously and unconsciously—we give our power away.

By orienting to a guiding purpose, we then have a compass to help us navigate our growth, fulfillment, and contentment—and the world we are hoping to contribute to creating. It's not about achieving a life purpose but rather living on purpose. When we are aligned with living on purpose, we can let go of the illusion of control and enjoy the flexibility and freedom of where we are as the emphasis of our attention and energy becomes more balanced between being and doing. For example, if we view our purpose as bringing content to the world and are thinking of creating a podcast, we might miss that it's actually meant to be a book or a blog or a vlog—which could be greater than ever imagined.

One of my favorite mantras, which came to me while meditating once, was *If I knew what it looked like, I'd miss what it is*. This gave me permission to let go and explore what was in my now, so that I could co-create with what the universe was providing, which is often a richer journey and outcome than we could craft for ourselves. If you may recall, I was set on building a framework for empathy. If I wasn't willing to let go of that, I may never have found the gifts of fear.

Let's connect to our assets to understand how we can best support ourselves through this process.

> *Nothing contributes so much to tranquilize the mind as a steady purpose—a point on which the soul may fix its intellectual eye.*
>
> —Mary Wollstonecraft Shelley

SEEDS TO PLANT

- Our authenticity is our freedom.
- Knowing our values helps us understand what triggers us.
- Our why can serve as our North Star.
- Our values are how we walk there.
- Being guided by our why plus walking our values enables us to live in integrity.
- Hope can serve as a reorientation from lack to abundance and is a doorway out of binary thinking and constructs.
- My why is bigger than I.
- Sometimes the thing we fear the most is being ourselves—which is what our fear is trying to help us do.

PART 3:

YOUR ASSETS

CHAPTER 10

SELF-AWARENESS: A TOOL TO ACCESS FREEDOM

All battles are first won, or lost, in the mind.
—Joan of Arc

Human beings are capable of observing their own thoughts while they're having them. What a gift! This becomes an entry point into change. *Self-awareness is the home of unstuck.*

As we looked at in the beginning of Part 2, anything we practice naturally increases. There's not a stagnant capacity of "it" that you can deplete—mental agility, physical agility, resilience, patience, and more. Most commonly, *x* begets more *x*. The same notion applies to choice. Every thought we have, every statement we make, we are practicing something. We might be practicing beneficial thinking.

We might be practicing self-limiting thoughts. The words we use and the thoughts we have create our realities. *We are practicing something all the time.* Our self-awareness gives us the ability to notice our practices, reflect on them, and ensure they're getting us closer to our truth and freedom.

THE ROLE OF THE OBSERVER

We have been conditioned to beat ourselves up mentally, but there's another way to live. If we can create space from looped self-critical thinking, we can shift our practice. The role of the observer is one of the most powerful roles we can inhabit. Being in the role of the observer:

- Gives helpful distance between the critical voice in your head and your true self
- Enables space for curiosity to evaluate our circumstances objectively
- Enables us to identify decision points
- Allows us to be present
- Allows us to respond intentionally instead of reacting unconsciously

Being the observer allows us to notice the space between reaction and response. We can begin to identify this space by creating pauses. The role of the observer is incredibly helpful by granting us access to reframing and new perspectives. We may not be able to choose our circumstances, but we can choose how we navigate through and respond to them.

Until you make the unconscious conscious, it will direct your life and you will call it fate.
—Carl Jung

While it's important to learn new practices that support our growth and intentionality, we need to unlearn the practices and patterns that are working against us. In fact, I think I spend more time with clients working on unlearning than learning. That's how impactful it is on us. To unlearn as defined by Merriam-Webster is "to undo the effect of or to put aside the practice of." Learning is defined as "gain[ing] knowledge of or skill in through study, instruction, or experience."

Unlearning and learning can happen at the same time.

If we think about how long we've been practicing subconscious, unconscious, and conscious fear, we've had the opportunity to become really good at it. Some of us are probably experts. It's about recognizing how we can engage our thoughts differently and become aware of what's happening subconsciously and automatically for us. In order to build new habits that promote intentional growth, we have to unlearn which patterns may be preventing us from recognizing our choice points. A great way to do this is to move into the role of the observer.

Let's revisit the neuroscience of decision-making. Every time we make a decision, we fire a neuron down a neural pathway. When we find ourselves in similar circumstances, making the same or similar decisions again and again, that neural pathway becomes a superhighway. When we hear someone say, "This always happens to me," or we find ourselves in a circumstance that happens all the time—this can be a clue that something worth exploring is going on in the subconscious. The effect of superhighways is that our brains are no longer able to recognize that there's a choice to be made. These pathways have fired so many times, the movement has become automatic (a reaction). Think of habits. If we have a behavior that isn't serving us—we've been practicing it on a loop because we fear pain and don't want that hurt to get triggered—we're going to react this way every single time to protect ourselves from the pain. Then we don't even have the choice to respond differently.

One of my clients recalls a presentation from a time in elementary school when she was ridiculed by some of her classmates. Over time, this caused her to become quiet and avoid sharing in group settings. Fast-forward, and she's now fairly new in her career at a Fortune 500 company. She has ideas to share and is often told by her manager she needs to speak up more, to be more vocal; she is able to do so in one-on-one settings. The superhighway created from getting quiet to protect herself was lodged into her subconscious, so she just shut down in group meetings. When we were able to identify the pattern and where it came from, we could connect her to what was true today so that she could make new choices and establish new neural pathways.

USING SELF-AWARENESS TO BRING INTENTIONALITY TO OUR RESPONSES

While our fear may be protecting us from reliving a previous pain, our situation now may not be the same. For instance, one of my clients is an overachiever. At a young age, she was severely scolded if she didn't deliver the highest and best (scores, ranks, etc.). In order to protect herself from pain, she delivered again and again as that was the way she obtained her parents' approval, or what may have felt like love. Over time, she also created a story that love was accomplishment. She was not consciously aware of this storyline. It was running in her subconscious, patterned by multiple experiences of being accepted after delivering the best. This story fueled her for many years and has served her in many ways. She is a senior executive at a highly regarded company who is proud of her many accomplishments. She's also exhausted and feeling trapped. She didn't know who she was without her achievements and accomplishments. Then she came to this realization and a new path forward presented itself.

When your worth is linked to your accomplishments, *your worth is linked to your accomplishments.* It's a never-ending cycle. Fear jumped in when my client's eight-year-old self was being scolded and made a promise to protect her from that pain and stayed committed to it. However, today she knows she is more than her accomplishments. And when we could open that door and begin to explore what is important to her—balance, spending more time with her family, reading a book for fun, exploring passions like traveling—she could begin to shift her relationship with her automatic doing—what had become her automatic form.

In order to make intentional choices, we first need to heighten our awareness. By becoming curious we can explore our fears—the role they've played in our lives as well as the information they have for us, enabling us to access our courage or let go of a story that is no longer relevant.

Let me give an example. Earlier we looked at the role of neural pathways and superhighways in decision-making. Unfortunately, vulnerability is often associated with weakness. It's what many of us were taught—or, more likely, what was modeled to many of us. Talk about a neuron on a superhighway: This is where unlearning and learning can happen at the same time. By connecting to what is true and disconnecting from what we adopted as true because of societal norms, constructs, or what previously had been true, we can start to unlearn the misperception that vulnerability is weakness while also creating a new neural pathway that associates vulnerability with strength. In this process we can practice moving away from binary thinking. It's not that vulnerability as a weakness ceases to exist immediately. While we're building the vulnerability-as-a-strength pathway, we can reinforce a new neural pathway by making choices that provide us the opportunity to practice vulnerability, which begins to enable our shift.

Here's an example from one of my clients who was able to dig beneath his trigger in order to access his vulnerability. This client was recently sharing a couple of challenging conversations he was having with his manager and director, which caused quite a bit of frustration. During the first conversation, they didn't ask my client for his ideas or opinions but rather told him what decisions they had come to and what they expected of him and his team. Based on his previous patterning, he reacted automatically by expressing strong frustration at this micromanaging approach, using terse language, and displaying standoffish body language, which was received as unprofessional. We talked about what was beneath his frustration. Why did he feel wronged? What was being misunderstood or not considered? Where was the tension? He shared that he was one of five children and often didn't feel heard growing up. He felt like he was being overlooked. This triggered his self-worth issues.

In the second conversation with his manager, he spoke directly to what was beneath the frustration and how challenging the situation was for him—that he wasn't feeling heard and that his ideas weren't even being considered, making him feel irrelevant. He also shared that even if his ideas weren't incorporated, a similar experience was being passed down through the team, creating a toxic environment. Much to his surprise, after sharing this vulnerability, the manager divulged the pressure that she and the director had been under. They were able to come to an agreement and create a new way forward—making room for all to share their ideas and opinions before finalizing a new path.

By modeling vulnerability as a strength, my client was able to give another—in this case, his manager—permission to practice the same approach. If he hadn't spent the time to practice self-awareness, to see what was beneath the trigger, he wouldn't have made this progress.

Pause. Take that in. By modeling another way, we give someone else permission to do the same. We create safety through our actions.

Modeling is the greatest form of leadership.

ACCESSING THE OBSERVER THROUGH OUR SELF-CRITIC

A fast way to become the observer is to get curious about the critical voice in our heads—an all-too-common voice for many of us. Remember my Gretchen from Part 1, who was the self-critical part of my makeup? Who's your Gretchen? What are they saying to you? What information are they pointing you to?

PRACTICE

A few tools for accessing the observer of our critical mind:

Nexting:

When your self-critic comes up—say "next" until you get to a nonjudgmental self-thought. Say this as many times as needed. You don't have to reach a positive place. It can be neutral.

Name your self-critic (mine was Gretchen):

When do they come around?

What are their playgrounds?

A couple of other possible observer access points:

Watch the circumstance you find yourself in, as if you're watching a movie. Narrate the scene. Notice how characters are behaving, including yourself.

Visualize a drone above you taking in all the information. Watch the scene play out.

By bringing our awareness to how often our self-critic comes around, we can become aware of its presence—a needed element for future shifts.

One of my clients is a founder of a start-up facing great pressure to successfully deliver upon his idea to his investors. Nexting proved to be incredibly useful as he navigated some of the more high-pressure moments:

I'm never going to find product market fit.

Next.

What if I run out of money?

Next.

I'm not going to be able to pay the team's salaries.

Next.

What if I fail?

Next.

I have to do the laundry. (Clearly, he was working remotely.)

Remember, the critic is not a terrible thing. It might even have relevant information for us—just not when it's playing on a loop ad nauseam. The important part of observing the critic is to create space so that you can choose how to engage for the information your self-critic has for you. Gretchen is an important part of me, and now when I see her coming, I can engage her to understand why she's here. Is she showing me what's important? If I have a big presentation coming up, is she making me question my value? Is she making me doubt my abilities? Is she protecting me from something? Maybe she's showing me it's important to rehearse. Perhaps it's to throw out the scripted talking points and have fun with the audience. Similar to engaging fear and the gifts it has to offer, Gretchen bringing my attention to something that I haven't considered makes the relationship with her a worthwhile one to cultivate and understand.

The fastest and easiest way to engage our critical thought is when we're not the thought itself (which we may feel like we are, if it's on a loop). Again, it's like we're watching a movie of ourselves versus being ourselves. Watching the script play out—our thoughts, emotional reactions, and so on—helps to create space. For instance, in my case, I might say, *Hmmm, Guryan's tone just shifted dramatically and she's starting to appear to be angry.* Or if in conversation with someone else, *Dana seems completely distracted and doesn't appear to be able to hear what I'm saying to her.* Both of these examples help to create a pause so that I can connect to what is beneath my building anger, or so that I can get curious about what Dana is going through rather than taking it personally and assuming what I'm saying isn't important to her.

PERSPECTIVE SPECTRUMS

This is where we can begin to consider what spectrums can make possible for us. Enter the world of what I refer to as "perspective spectrums." While they may appear to be opposites, I look at them instead as spectrums of wholeness. As I reviewed earlier with the spectrum of fear and courage, spectrums allow us to see where there's a place to shift, presuming we can move into the observer's role and bring our awareness to doing so.

Spectrums can be subjective. What's at one end of your spectrum might be different from another person's or from the ones I list here. Many are based on our experiences and patterns. If you are finding yourself in one place—for instance, a place of judgment—ask yourself what the other end of that spectrum is for you?

Connection	⇔	Disconnection
Certainty	⇔	Uncertainty
Judgmental	⇔	Curious
Fear	⇔	Courage
Micro	⇔	Macro
Adaptable	⇔	Intractable
Apathetic	⇔	Compassionate

Rather than relating to an either/or binary stance, what if you could find your own continuums? They don't have to be binary. In fact, they rarely are. I can experience fear and courage simultaneously. I can be judgmental while I allow that to serve as a signal and inform me to move into a space of curiosity to learn more. In this case, my judgment serves as the cue for me to get curious.

In another example of shifting to perspective-spectrum thinking, I was deeply afraid to leave my marriage. I could tell you a story about how I was afraid to be alone, to have nothing but unknowns in front of me. I could also tell a story about how courageous it was to leave my marriage, to move into the unknowns. I learned to trust that everything in my life had come from unknowns, and that fear itself was convincing me that unknowns are something to fear. Courage doesn't come from neutrality—it comes from fear. Fear has a hold on us when we are holding our breath, but we can choose to exhale and move into our courage. If we think about every courageous decision we've made, what we likely felt right before it was our fear.

Spectrums allow for adaptation—the ability to evolve to meet our current environment. Sometimes this can be by choice and other times not. Take sheltering in place during the COVID pandemic, for example. So many of my clients made statements like "I'll be okay if it's only two more weeks." Or "I'm fine as long as they keep the parks open and there's access to nature." Or "I can't stay at home with my family all day every day—I'll go crazy." Still, all of them adapted. Those who felt victimized, however, had a harder time of it. Those who looked for opportunities found a way to grow. They learned about patience, they started to garden at home, they found new things to appreciate in their family and the importance of spending time with themselves. In this case, we weren't given the choice to adapt, but in most circumstances, this choice is ours to make.

A spectrum allows for options and the ability to increase our awareness to make intentional choices. If we allow our circumstances to inform us, we have the option of shifting in a new direction. If we are all the way on one side of a continuum, we may be digging in our heels. Think of this spectrum: Is this happening *to* me or is this happening *for* me? This spectrum might look like:

Victim ⇔ Growth

How can looking at your life through a different perspective give you the ability to reframe it?

Another personal example of how I chose to view my experience through the growth-victim lens is as follows. I am partly driven by my passions. For about a decade in my life, that manifested as working for companies that were trying to make the world a better place—that were making a difference. These employers helped move cars off internal combustion engines and oil, bring education to every human being around the globe, and create resilient communities for disaster preparedness, mitigation, and recovery. I ended up choosing to leave each for different reasons, but many had swayed from their original promise. It's challenging for a company to stay true to its core values and purpose when there's a fear of meeting a bottom line (and there's a way to stay committed to the bottom line, but that's for another time). In this case, I was at the third company where I was ready to commit two years of my life to traveling to third-world countries to help build resilient communities in preparation for disasters. I had started preparing for my departure, even said some goodbyes. Then, only two weeks prior to departure, it became clear that the company and I had different standards for my safety. I had to resign. I was crushed. *Why did this happen to me?* was my closed-in mindset.

Not only was I looking forward to this opportunity—to have the ability to make a difference in the world—it also had become part of my ego and identity. I could tell people legitimately that I was going to make a difference in the world. A lot was tied up here for me—internally and externally. How could I stomach the bruising to my ego? How could I have failed (again) to have found a company that was truly making a difference?

After working through the initial disappointment, identity crisis, confusion, and pain, they all became my impetus to do something differently. I was tired of quitting. I wanted to help leaders operate from a position of integrity, and to understand what kept people from wanting to live in integrity. This began my journey to build my work with coaching and leadership training around fear, which is one of the greatest gifts of my life. It makes me feel alive. Why did it happen for me? Repeated resignations due to my own frustrations connected me to the truest expression of my being.

It's not easy. It's hard. Even harder in the long term is keeping a victim mindset of *Why is this happening to me?* Sometimes we need to make this discovery in hindsight. When things feel challenging, the why-is-this-happening-for-me framing gives us a way to navigate those initial steps with trust and openness. We do so with curiosity about what more will be revealed as we continue to stay open to the lesson and our growth unfolding in front of us.

If we find ourselves digging in our heels on one side of the spectrum (e.g., disconnection), can we pause and get curious about what the other end of the spectrum (e.g., connection) holds for us? By doing so, we can begin to identify the space to see and understand our options and decide if shifting on the spectrum would serve us. For instance, if we find ourselves in a place of judgment, can we pause and ask ourselves, *What can I get curious about?* Judgments typically come with a story, an assumption we are making. Becoming curious about *why* we're feeling judgmental enables us to arrive at a useful understanding that can shift our perspective. Let's take a look at this in practice.

One of my clients is in a senior management position. As in many companies, after COVID she had to navigate the world of the hybrid work environment and the challenge of getting employees to return to the office. One employee in particular had quite a difficult time. She would come in late and leave early, if she came at all. My client and I had many conversations about her frustration with and judgments about this employee: how she was taking advantage of the circumstance, how she wasn't putting her colleagues first, and how selfish she was being. However, when my client turned judgment into curiosity, she was able to discover that this employee was navigating severe health issues, and moreover was a very private person so wasn't revealing this information willingly. The larger issue overrode whether the employee handled the situation correctly. For the purpose of our learning, we want to recognize when we're being judgmental so that we can pivot to curiosity. *How will my circumstance lead me to a solution more efficiently and effectively—and that takes both people into consideration?*

There isn't just one way to navigate our circumstances. The approach I suggest would be to remain open to all the useful information around us so that we can choose the path that serves us best. From that point, we can go on connecting to our values and practicing behaviors that are true to our purposeful way of being.

SHOULDS ARE RED FLAGS

Another signal to be aware of is "shoulding" yourself. Shoulds are a common tactic of fear and often a slightly more subtle tool in fear's arsenal. We have all been practicing shoulds since the day we became too old to have that make-believe friend or pretend world we explored, when it was time for us to know better. We *should* act like good girls and boys. We *should* go to this college. We *should* take that job. We *should* wear what's popular. We *should* get married and have children. The shoulds go on and on.

While it may not apply 100 percent of the time, try bringing your curiosity to the point at which you hear yourself *should* yourself. Take a moment. Think about it. Are you shoulding yourself? Is this why you chose your career path? Where to live? What to wear? What to invest your time in? Because success is so narrowly defined and rejection is so terrifying for many, we often should ourselves into a path that isn't based on our own contentment. A good place to start is defining what success means to you. Does it include freedom, balance, creative expression, community? What brings you contentment?

What if we apply our curiosity to the *role* that shoulds play in our lives? Like many things on repeat, we may not even hear the shoulds because of our repeated subconscious practice of following them. An interesting way to see how present shoulds might be is to start using the word "no."

For readers who are people-pleasers, this challenge might seem a bridge too far. When you say no, you free yourself to start a new practice and thus forge a new neural pathway.

What if you could discover your true yeses?

> ## PRACTICE
> ## LET'S DISCOVER YOUR YESES
>
> For the time being, say "no" to everything you're asked to do. (Take a moment to pause and do this internally.) You don't need to communicate this no externally at first.
>
> Then ask yourself, *Is this a true yes for me?*
>
> If so, why?
>
> Who are you saying yes for? You? Someone else?
>
> What does it bring to them?
>
> What does saying yes bring to you? (Understanding the answer to this last question is important to connect you to your true yeses.)
>
> You may not be able to outwardly say no to everything immediately. You can still use this practice to start discovering what your yeses are.

As this applies to the workplace or personal relationships, if you find yourself in a circumstance where true expression and growth aren't present, consider why you are there and if quitting the job or relationship would open new doors for you. I don't put a negative connotation around quitting. Saying no to a box, a construct, or a should might be the first door opening to saying yes to your true self.

One final point here. Once you find your yeses, I recommend putting boundaries in place to support your ability to use them. An important point about your boundaries is that you're the only one who holds them. For instance, if you decide you want to have fifty-minute rather than one-hour meetings (or twenty-five minutes rather than thirty), you're the one who has to hold that boundary, not the other people in the meeting.

The only person who can be responsible for holding your boundaries is you.

SEEDS TO PLANT

- We are what we practice and we're practicing something all the time.
- Self-awareness is the home of unstuck.
- Unlearning and learning can happen at the same time.
- Modeling is the greatest form of leadership.
- Being the observer creates space and allows us to open to the new.
- Notice if you're shoulding yourself.
- Everything comes from the unknown. Just like you, the unknown gets lonely too–and wants to be discovered.

CHAPTER 11

THE POWER OF PAUSE

Between stimulus and response there is a space.
In that space is our power to choose our response. In our
response lies our growth and our freedom.
—Viktor E. Frankl

Over years of coaching, I have developed numerous exercises to help people unwire patterns that are no longer serving them so that they can move into choice and intentional living. As I developed these exercises, I kept them in a master document. When I searched, the word that appeared more than any other, by a landslide, was "pause."

UNLEARNING IS ESSENTIAL TO LEARNING

Learning new tools, approaches, and practices is a necessary and incredibly supportive part of the change process. We must also unlearn, unwire, and repattern previous behaviors and thought forms that aren't serving us, or else they remain fixed. Otherwise, these new learnings simply act as Band-Aids, protecting us from old patterns if not provoked, which is unrealistic. These new learnings might even work most of the time. But we are triggered when an old pain is provoked or when a value is threatened—when it really counts—and our old pattern can reemerge and run the show if we haven't taken the time to unwire and unlearn that pattern.

Pausing enables us to use our powers of self-awareness and observation to choose to engage differently. Pauses create the space needed to unwire automatic reactions. In the previous chapter we spoke about engaging your Gretchen, the self-critic, in a way that enables you to derive value from the relationship. In order to do so, we first create space so that we have time to engage in this new way. When you pause, slow down, and distance yourself from a reaction you may have to a situation, you are creating space.

Space is where choice can be applied, allowing an important shift to take place. When we pause, we can practice curiosity. What fear reaction are you noticing? Are you holding your breath, experiencing tunnel vision, biting your pen? What is beneath the trigger? What pain did this awaken? Are you feeling overlooked or underappreciated? What value isn't being honored?

If conviction is a value for you and you feel you have been misled or lied to, how are you pausing in that moment to see if you can connect with what is true—for you or who you feel has wronged you? What's most important for you to connect to and maybe consider conveying to the other, from a place of intention? Unwiring the automatic can be complicated—and the automatic can be powerful because we've had a lot of practice with it. Looking at the conscious and subconscious mind can be helpful.

HOW PAUSING BECOMES OUR DOORWAY TO UNLEARNING

As defined by Merriam-Webster, "conscious" means all thoughts and actions within our awareness—for example, the beauty and pleasantness of a red rose's smell. And subconscious is an entry point to all reactions and automatic actions we can become aware of if we think about them. Consider our ability to drive a car: Once we are skilled at it, we stop thinking which gears to use, which pedals to press, or which mirror to look at, yet we can always become aware of what we're doing once we consciously think about it. As a result, if we raise our attention through the power of observation, we can make the subconscious conscious, thereby engaging our ability to rewire old patterns.

Pausing can provide a key to our subconscious.

I discovered the power of pause early into my coaching as I was surprised by how often it came up. I take notes for all my clients, partly so they can stay present and not have to worry about focusing on note-taking. I began to notice that introducing the practice of pausing came up during the majority of conversations—and still does. Before we could talk about what new mindsets to practice (like turning toward the critic) or what models of communication should be used for hard conversations (like giving feedback, which is incredibly challenging for so many), we had to see what pattern was causing my client to react a certain way (avoiding the critic, shutting down, running imposter syndrome stories, etc.).

One of the surprises of this powerful practice is that it needs to last only a moment, the length of a breath, to stop an automatic reaction. And even though it's taken years to hard wire these patterns, the more we pause, the faster we can create space to respond intentionally. It does not take the same amount of time to lodge these patterns into our subconscious as it takes to unwire them. Pausing increases the rate of unwiring by ensuring that we're not letting our subconscious lead our decision-making.

> ## PRACTICE
>
> Building pauses into our days is an incredibly helpful practice that creates spaces for engaging moments intentionally versus from a place of reaction. You can practice this proactively, without a trigger serving as the catalyst.
>
> Proactive Pause:
>> Build in three two-minute pauses during your day. One might be mid-workday, one might be before transitioning into your evening. When you pause, ask yourself,
>> - When I think about my next _____ (meeting, visit, evening with kids, etc.), what is most important to me? How do I want to show up?
>> - Do I need to let go of or clear anything, so that I don't take it with me to what's next?
>
> Trigger Pause:
>> The moment you notice feeling triggered (angry, frustrated, short-fused, withdrawing, etc.), pause and ask yourself,
>> - What feeling is beneath this trigger reaction (hurt, insulted, overlooked, etc.)?
>> - What value is being threatened? What value can I connect to and bring forth within me or to my circumstances?
>> - What is most important about the value you have just connected to?

Habits are hard to break, and as I keep pointing out, they're also hard to start. Whenever I have started a new habit, I've written reminders on Post-it notes (something powerful resides in the tactile nature of a Post-it note) and put them all over the place. In addition to that trusty approach, I've set meeting alarms on my phone as reminders. I've asked for accountability partners.

In order to set yourself up for successfully adopting a new habit, ask yourself what can work for you to help support your accountability.

When beginning any new practice, it's a good reminder to practice some self-compassion in order to set yourself up for successful shifting. I think the most powerful habit we can develop and practice is to pause. Get out your Post-it notes!

Practice takes practice.

SEEDS TO PLANT

The most important word in the English language is "pause."

CHAPTER 12

BODY AS INFORMER

Our bodies communicate to us clearly and specifically, if we are willing to listen to them.

—Shakti Gawain

More great news: We have more knowledge within our bodies than many of us realize. When we bring our self-awareness to our body's signals, we are given the cues needed to stop, shift out of involuntary reactive behavior, shift into conscious, deliberate responses, and begin to unwire old patterns that no longer serve.

When our brain thinks we're in danger, it prepares its stress reactions: fight, flight, freeze, or fawn. Our bodies are tense when we're in that mode. Our palms may get sweaty, our body may seize up, we may get a stomachache. These signals—cues—can appear differently for each of us. Again, this happens to protect us. Our breath likely becomes short and fast. Our mind is outside itself, perhaps playing out a worst-case scenario or on overload playing out all the worst-case scenarios we can imagine.

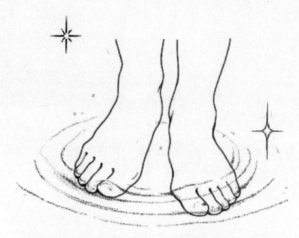

OUR BODIES AS TUNING FORKS

How can we leverage our body's responses, which often may feel or look like the shadow attributes associated with fear: fight, flight, freeze, fawn?

We can let our bodies be our tuning forks. Our bodies have so much information for us. For example, if fear is your fierce protector, your intuition is your loyal guardian of truth. When we're sitting with someone and the experience is fulfilling and enriching, our stomach probably feels relaxed; we're breathing calmly and deeply. We may even be leaning in, feeling light and completely unaware of how much time has passed. When we're doing something that is aligned with our truth—sometimes referred to as the "flow state"— we may feel alive, invigorated, spacious. If something is triggering us or may just not be a true yes for us, we're more likely to experience some tension or a sense of being closed in. Our breathing is definitely shallower. If we're shoulding ourselves into doing something for someone else, we may feel irritable and tight-chested, and find ourselves often wondering what time it is.

Just like fingerprints, every body is different. We may all have different ways of developing a line to our intuition. Our body speaks and knows our language. Think about the gut feeling we have when we know something is the way to go, even if the external signs may not point in that direction. This is an invitation to learn the language of you. What are your signals? What do yeses feel like in your body? What do nos feel like? Where do they present themselves? In your breath? Your shoulders? Your jaw? Your attitude? Your relationship with time? What else?

> ## REFLECTION
>
> Think of a time when you have had an unconscious reaction to fear (fight, flight, freeze, fawn).
>
> Bring your awareness to "the build"—the increasing intensity of the anger, the ignoring of needs to please another, the shutting down to avoid conflict. . . .
>
> What cues does your body give you right before you slip into subconscious reaction? Examples: Do you clench your jaw, hold your breath, bite on a straw? Do your ears get hot? What else?
>
> As soon as you notice any of these cues . . .
>
> *PAUSE*
>
> Get curious *(How can I engage this moment differently?)*:
> - What is this moment trying to tell you?
> - What is being threatened? What are you protecting?
> - How do you want to engage at this moment?
> - Which of your values can you embody?
> - If you're on one side of a perspective spectrum, how might the other end provide a new framing?
> - What reaction do you observe, and what response would you prefer to choose?

Practice with your body being your tuning fork. What signals is it trying to send you? What cues can you observe before you start slipping into unhelpful beliefs and behaviors? It's more than just body language, which can serve as an outward expression. What's happening within also shows us when fear is present. We have trained ourselves so intently to avoid fear that we generally don't recognize the cues until they escalate from sensation to behavior. Then suddenly we're not just feeling fear, we're reacting out of fear in a subconscious flight, fight, freeze, or fawn reaction (we're screaming at our partner, appeasing someone when we're out of all capacity, storming out, and so on). Whatever it is, we tend to know after the emotional reaction has become so obvious as to manifest in an automatic action.

At first, it can be hard to know in the moment. What's even harder—and critically important for unlearning—is to begin to recognize the cues *before* the reaction occurs. What's more, the signal our body has for us is the very way to recognize a reaction is coming. The cues present themselves as you unconsciously build toward the reaction. The more we understand and learn to recognize our unique cues in the moment, the more we can swiftly bring awareness to our behavior and then choose to respond to the signals differently.

Additionally, we have available to us ways to engage and receive information from our bodies if we are open to exploring them. We're taught early about the five senses: touch, taste, smell, feel, and hearing. We aren't taught some other senses—those based more in energetics, or the study of flow and transformation of energy—that also have insights for us and additional ways to learn about how our bodies are communicating to us. Many of the ways our bodies make us aware of information are quite subtle, and most of us never learned explicitly about their presence.

GROUNDING–CENTERING

Our ability to engage and receive the information our body has for us increases when we're in our center—and I haven't found anything that brings us into our center more than grounding. Grounding is a coping approach designed to connect you immediately with the present moment.

These techniques can be helpful with a variety of types of anxiety—as well as in navigating daily life. Grounding techniques are often used as a way of coping with flashbacks or dissociation when a person has posttraumatic stress disorder (PTSD).[4] When we're in fear, we're either in the future, what-if-ing ourselves, or in the past, judging and shaming ourselves. But when we are present, we can choose how we want to navigate that moment and the decisions available to us. Grounding becomes an essential tool in helping connect us to the present. Many grounding exercises are available.

Many of my clients work in high-paced, high-intensity jobs. They might go hours without taking an intentional deep breath, contributing to their sense of busyness, overwhelm, and stress. I was on a video call with one of my clients who works from home, and she was what could only be described as in a spin. She was frantically explaining to me what she had to get taken care of for work and her kid's needs, that there wasn't enough time, and that she would be working late after dinner again. I noticed some grass outside her window. I asked her to get off the call, take her shoes off, put a three-minute timer on, and go walk back and forth on the grass. I gave her two rules. She had to set her phone down, close enough to where she could hear the alarm, and she was to keep her focus on two sensations: what the bottom of her feet felt like on the grass and her breath. When she returned, her entire system had shifted. She was calm and felt regulated, and we were then able to move into a productive conversation—all because of a three-minute pause.

This is just one example of how to ground. In the Practice text below are some other tips I share with my clients. As always, some work for some people while others work for others. The key is to find practices that work for you.

PRACTICE

Grounding helps us connect to the present moment by bringing our awareness to sensations that help us get back in our bodies. When we are thinking about the future or past, we are in our heads and outside the present moment. Here are some options for practicing grounding:

- Feel your sacral bone on the seat, with your feet below you grounded into the earth or floor.
- Notice your breath.
  - Exhale all the breath in your body.
  - Notice where you're starting from.
  - Take three deep breaths at each level:
    - Breathe down to breastbone
    - Breathe down to diaphragm
    - Breathe down to pubic bone
- Walk in your bare feet on natural ground (grass, dirt, sand).
- Take a bath and wash down the drain all that weighs on your mind.
- Get into nature—the woods; near, on, or in water; a mountaintop; a park—wherever you can access it.
- Realize that nature speaks a language all its own—one that any of us can understand. What messages does nature hold for you?

The next couple of recommendations fall under what I'm going to call "practical woo." I'll state up front: I am a skeptical person, and my skepticism becomes my discernment. What do I mean by that? If I'm trying a new approach, practice, or methodology, I'm likely going to be skeptical as I begin. If it doesn't end up resonating or benefiting me, then perhaps my skepticism was helpful. However, if the something new does resonate and shows me a new practice that's helpful for me, my skepticism pivots to my discernment, allowing me to shift my opinion based on my new knowledge. I am really opinionated, but if given a good reason, I'll shift my opinion. What's the downside to exploring? In service of navigating your youness and your trueness, get your skepticism ready.

THE FOUR BODIES: A WAY OF ENGAGING

Thinking of experiences through the five senses is limiting. For instance, you know that feeling you get when you know someone is staring at you? Even if they're behind you? That's energy—a sense worthy of greater exploration. And the five senses don't cover it.

We're not just bystanders to our bodies. We can be active participants. How can we engage the information our bodies offer? First, it's helpful to have a frame so that we can access a more holistic version of ourselves.

I like to think each of us has four bodies in the form of spheres. For me, starting in closest to me is my physical body. Then, moving outward, are my emotional body, my mental body, and my energetic body. This outlook gives me a way to be my own observer. I'll consider, *If I am experiencing fear, which of the four bodies might be a doorway into exploring what fear is present and how my body is trying to alert me?*

In an ideal world, all my bodies are in balance—yet that's rarely the case. If we imagine four bodies in a car, generally someone is in the driver's seat. If I'm swimming, my physical body might be the driver. If I'm meditating, it's my energetic body. If I'm ideating, my mental body is the operator. When I'm actively grieving, my emotional body is in control.

Our bodies can be incredible tools when trying to bring balance to our circumstances if we feel out of sorts. For instance, if our mind seems to be racing out of control, our mind probably won't be what brings us back into balance. However, another of the three bodies could serve us in a balancing role. If our mind is racing, how might we bring another body into the driver's seat? Here are some examples:

Physical: Can you take a deep breath? Notice where your breath is reaching within you. Can you breathe it in more fully? Can you exercise? Shake out your arms or legs? Get a massage?

Emotional: Is there a feeling you're resisting? Is there sadness or anger or frustration or desire or _____ (fill in the blank) that's wanting to be felt?

Mental: When dealing with irrational fear, the mental body is often out of balance, so using that mental body won't help much.

That said, fear offers a great opportunity to tune into our curiosity and ask these two powerful questions:

What is true?

What am I telling myself is true?

Energetic: Can you meditate or listen to a guided meditation? Can you shift the energy in your space (e.g., open a window, spray rosewater, light sage or palo santo)? Breathing works here too.

When we start to expand the ways we have of bringing ourselves into balance, we give ourselves more opportunity to practice our awareness and return to the present moment. We might also learn how we truly feel about something that we may not have previously noticed because another one of our bodies was distracting us from it, maybe even at the nudging of fear to protect us.

To demonstrate this, I'll share an example from a client who has recently been on an active exploration to discover his truth as he found he had adopted many constructs that defined success that weren't his. His mental body was starting to use imposter-syndrome tactics to try to convince him to stay in his corporate track. He began to attune to his emotional and energetic bodies and merely asked, *What do I truly want?* The answer didn't come in that moment. He continued to ask the question and started to notice what the other bodies were telling him. They led him to his truth: that he wanted to start a business with his family—and now that's what he's doing.

One other beautiful thing about this process is . . .

The truth of who we are and what we want runs so deeply that it manifests itself not only in our conscious thought but in our subconscious bodies. Our physical selves are in cahoots with our deeper truth, which conspires to send us clues to

The mystery of what's really going on inside of us is a mystery that wants to be solved.

explore. So when your body is sending you signals you don't understand (maybe you are getting headaches, you keep stubbing your toe, you can't kick the feeling of being tired, or you don't feel truly alive when you're doing something), follow that thread. See where it leads. It looks different for everyone. Once you discover a deeper truth you want to remember, watch for the cues that you're about to slide into subconscious behaviors that you're trying to avoid. Pay attention to those signals. They're happening for a reason.

PRACTICE
PLAYING WITH THE FOUR BODIES

We are more than just our thoughts and our physical bodies. Expand the way you can access information about yourself by exploring all four bodies:

- Physical
- Emotional
- Mental
- Energetic

How can your awareness of the roles these four bodies can play support you?

- Be aware of balance and imbalance.
- Who's in the driver seat?
- Who could help bring balance to the circumstance?
- Where is your own deeper truth playing a role in your shift?
- Where in your body is the truth giving you cues to explore?

The more we understand what's happening in our bodies, the more we can learn when something physical is guiding us back to our presence so that we can navigate our situations with intentionality.

THE CLAIRES— A WAY OF RECEIVING

We have a GPS (global positioning system) on our phone that guides us. Within us, we have a PGS system—our personal gut system—that can also guide us if we allow it. PGS is another name for intuition. Fear and intuition are guiding us to the same place; intuition is showing us the path, and fear is trying to scare us from that very path.

A gut feeling is a powerful guide. When you have that gut feeling that causes you to do or not do something, to go somewhere or not, to trust someone or something or not—that's our intuition giving us a message. I have found a few ways we can receive these messages. Enter what I refer to as "the Claires":

Clairvoyance: The ability to see with the mind's eye

Clairaudience: The power or faculty of hearing something not present to the ear but regarded as having objective reality

Clairsentience: The ability to sense physical, emotional, and energy in the form of seemingly unearthly scents, touches, and movements (may manifest as goose bumps)

Claircognizance: The ability to know something without using your sense of logic

Any one person is unlikely to have all these, but I have worked with and witnessed people who have each of the Claires. Some people I work with have visions; they may see an image of a person and then end up meeting that person on a date. Others hear messages; they might be guided to sign up for an event and then end up meeting the perfect person for their network.

Sometimes people have more than one Claire. The two that are strongest for me are clairsentience and claircognizance. In fact, when a client shares something with me during a video meeting that is so powerful it gives me goose bumps, I lift my arm up on the video screen so they can see my hairs standing on edge. That's how important what they just shared with me was, and I want to make sure they heard this. I actually believe that what we say out loud is mostly for that very reason, so we can hear it. Remember, our fear and our intuition are pointing us to the same place—our intuition by leading us to our truth, our fear by scaring us about that very thing. Learning the language of our Claires can turn up the volume of the call to our truth, which offers another way to quiet our fear.

Which Claire, if any, is on your team? If you don't have a connection to any of them, it may take some time. Remember those boxes we consciously or unconsciously started jumping into when we were younger? At that time, each jump made our connection to our intuition a little more distant. Our gut may even have been sending us messages or signals, and we probably ignored them. If you had been ignored for years, or even decades, you also might give up trying. But the good news is that our intuitions are ready to come back. And the best part? They don't hold grudges, so invite yours. They might welcome the connection. I have witnessed this repeatedly with countless clients. Once we can learn the language of our bodies and recognize how it's trying to get our attention (goose bumps, a chill down the neck, aliveness, stuckness, etc.), we can pause and practice a new way that serves who we truly are.

I've been told many times in my life, typically by people older than I am, "People don't change. They are who they are." I wholeheartedly disagree. And I don't think this comes from a place of naivety. I see people change daily.

In fact, I'm graced with the gift of working with those I refer to as the "mascots of change." Anyone who is interested in being one can be.

People who want to change, who choose to change, can change.

Be patient with the process, allow the body to do its work, and support yourself with love and the knowledge that everything is changing all the time. A living organism seeks to grow.

SEEDS TO PLANT

- Let your body be your tuning fork.
- Your body knows your language. Allow it to connect more fully to your intuition.
- How are you practicing engaging and receiving information from your body?
- What cues does your body send you before you slip into a subconscious reaction?
- If you want to change and practice ways to support that change, you can.
- Remember to listen to the little cues before your body starts throwing migraines or gastrointestinal issues your way.

CHAPTER 13

THE INFLUENCE OF STORYTELLING

*We don't see things the way they are,
we see them the way we are.*

—Anaïs Nin

Storytelling is not just a powerful communication tool, though we can look to its power in various places such as religion, business, and government. Storytelling actually has a neurological impact on our brains. The *Harvard Business Review* published the following in an article titled "The Science Behind the Art of Storytelling":

> Scientists are discovering that chemicals like cortisol, dopamine and oxytocin are released in the brain when we're told a story. Why does that matter? If we are trying to make a point stick, cortisol assists with our formulating memories. Dopamine, which helps regulate our emotional responses, keeps

us engaged. When it comes to creating deeper connections with others, oxytocin is associated with empathy, an important element in building, deepening or maintaining good relationships.

Perhaps most importantly, storytelling is central to meaning-making and sense-making. It is through story that our minds form and examine our own truths and beliefs, as well as discern how they correlate with the truths and beliefs of others. Through story listening, we gain new perspectives and a better understanding of the world around us. We challenge and expand our own understanding by exploring how others see and understand the world through their lens.

I love the concept of story listening. I wrote before of the importance of being mindful with what words you say and what thoughts you let run. What are the stories you're telling yourself? What are their messages? How does the story narrate your day? Your life?

What is the impact of our storytelling? Our identity is deeply tied into our narrative of ourselves—our stories—which often includes protecting us from becoming the next, renewed version of ourselves. This is because fear knows how to protect us here—where we currently are: in our comfort zone. As soon as we begin to shift or even think about shifting into new practices or directions, our fear may get louder because it doesn't know how to protect us in new environments. I think this is where "the devil you know" got its legs.

Remember, rational fears are those that present a risk to our survival. They're in the present moment. This might be the wind moving patio furniture outside, which sounds like an intruder. Irrational fears live in the future tense and are the what-if scenarios we are creating through the stories in our minds. When we're in unhealthy fear, we are in an assumption. We are running a what-if, future-tense scenario. For example: *What if there is a lockdown at my children's school tomorrow? What if I fail that certification test?* We are telling ourselves a story that may not be grounded in facts or reflective of our current reality, or what we actually want (our yes).

Doing the work isn't a light switch we can flip. It takes time. It takes, well, doing the work. It's a way of eating and exercising versus taking a diet pill. Moving from blaming others and victimization to personal responsibility and forgiveness takes time. This practice also requires unlearning old patterns and thought forms that don't serve you well while also learning new ways of being. The process gives us access to feeling what we may not have previously allowed ourselves to feel from old pains or traumas—so there may be some releasing that's needed.

If you're in a self-critical spiral, you can use the previously shared tool of nexting or pausing to get curious about what is true versus what you're telling yourself is true. Consider it counterprogramming. You can also notice the finality of your stories and what you might be claiming. For instance, if you claim you can't do something (communicate in a certain way, find a partner, etc.), then you probably won't be able to. You can use supportive language to help you bridge between where you are and where you want to go.

As an example, one of my clients who originally came to me with a lot of insecurity around the way he communicated was able to change the narrative of his story: *Up until now, it has been difficult for me to communicate effectively as I wasn't equipped with the tools to do so. Going forward, I am building my tool kit to enable effective communication.* Another option is adding "for now" to the end of a sentence—opening the possibility for a shift. I am in a creative rut, *for now*. I feel stuck, *for now*. I am having a hard time with my partner, *for now*.

Finally, remember that one of the hallmarks of storytelling is casting roles. This is helpful to see if you have a pattern. Do you always cast yourself in the same kind of role? We typically cast ourselves and the people around us into one of three roles—victim, villain, or hero. I had a bad day, and bad things happened to me—I'm a victim. I had a bad day, I really screwed up, and it's all my fault—I'm a villain. I had an amazing day, and I did amazing things—I'm a hero. Being aware of what role you've taken on can help serve as a doorway to a new perspective. Like perspective spectrums, if you perceive yourself as a victim or a hero, how would the story have been different if you played a different role?

We aren't limited to these three roles. It can be difficult to break out of a cycle of victimhood or villainy, but just as troublesome can be the need to always be the hero. It might be nice to hang up the cape and take a day off. Remember that there are a few more roles available to you in the story of your day. I had a bad day, and I'm curious to understand what the hell is up with me—I'm a detective. I had a bad day, and I could really use some self-care—I'm a friend. Or . . . I had a bad day, and I just need to acknowledge how I'm feeling—I'm a witness to my own unfolding and continued development.

STORYTELLING DIRECTLY IMPACTS OUR IDENTITY

Whatever roles we choose to cast ourselves in, it's usually more helpful to *choose the role mindfully* rather than falling back into old, subconscious habits. So read the script of your story with a critical eye, and don't be afraid to play casting director and switch up the roles once in a while. If nothing else, it will help you avoid typecasting yourself as the victim or the villain.

Our brains aren't invested in what's best for us. They're like massive data centers, validating the data we feed it. We have a choice in the reality we are creating for ourselves. *We're literally telling our brains what reality to validate and make manifest.* If we have this power, then we might as well use it to create the world we desire to see. When we do make shifts and step into more intentional decision-making, it's equally important to honor these shifts from a storytelling perspective as well. The stories we tell ourselves affect our identity. They are so powerful that if we don't rewrite them to reflect our now, they can keep us connected to an outdated identity.

> *The words we use and thoughts we have create our reality.*

For example, I often see clients who tell me they have imposter syndrome while simultaneously taking risks and leading teams. Or they tell me they're scared to have an honest conversation when they just shared the three most recent examples of how they practiced their vulnerability. The previous story they had about being an imposter or scared to expose themselves isn't congruent with their current identity. We've run the stories in our heads so many times, we have to replace those stories with new ones that reflect the current version of ourselves.

PRACTICE

We want to become aware of the stories we are telling ourselves and begin to practice stories that support the life we want to create.

Upgrading stories: When you notice a story from your past that limits you, pause and write down your old story and your new story.

Here's an example from one of my clients:

- **Old story regarding exercise:** I was being forced to do it. It caused arguments. It was a point of contention between me and my parents. It was frustrating.
- **New story regarding exercise:** I enjoy it. I am doing it and it has a positive impact on my life. It increases the quality of my life.

If you're feeling ready for the graduate practice, try the following:

When you notice your mind is running the old story, pause, use nexting to unwire the old story, and practice running the new story.

Claiming and honoring who you are today helps cellularize it in your body and your mind. Say it to yourself. Say it out loud. What's one of the fastest ways to cellularize it? Say it looking into your eyes in the mirror. *I am leading my team with confidence. I am welcoming challenges and new ideas. I enjoy thinking outside the box. I am presenting with poise. I am sharing my vulnerability as a way to connect with others more deeply.* And remember, you likely repeated the old story multiple times, and you will need to do it with your new story. Repeat your new truth, often.

What if a mindset of abundance makes a different future possible? *If we're telling ourselves stories, we may as well choose to tell ourselves stories that benefit us.* Understanding the cause of the story that isn't benefiting us can also be helpful. Stories live in the future or the past. The choice, however, is in this present moment.

SEEDS TO PLANT

- Our identity is deeply rooted in the stories we tell ourselves.
- If we're telling ourselves stories, we may as well tell stories that serve us.
- Choice lives in the present moment.
- The stories we tell ourselves shape how we see ourselves.
- Remember to choose to play the role you want to play in your own story.

PART 4:
THE INVITATION

CHAPTER 14

YOUR UNIQUE PATTERNING

If you always do what you've always done, you'll always get what you've always got.
—Henry Ford

Patterning affects our decision-making, often in subconscious ways because our patterns influence our automatic ways of being.

I'm not saying that you always cause your own pain. Because we fear fear and we fear pain and we never, or rarely, consider their role in how we navigate life and make decisions, we are complicit in creating patterns without even realizing we are doing so. We experienced moments of pain and fear with a desire to protect ourselves. Since then, with repeated practice, we have been unconsciously lodging beliefs, stories, and perceptions into our subconscious.

We play a part in creating our patterns.

Some people may have a direct line of communication with their intuition and are receiving messages as to where they want to grow and expand. For others, fear serves the same role, by showing us where we want to grow and expand. What matters most, though, is *what* we seek to grow. The unknown that we grow into reveals what's possible. We cannot grow without unknowns. *By making us scared, fear brings our attention to the very unknown we seek to explore.* It's just ironic that fear's only language is fear—so we turn away from it instead of toward it. In this case, fear can serve as a compass, showing you where to apply your courage in service of your growth.

What if we could rewrite our story and unwire the pattern that tells us to fear the unknown, and instead view the unknown with openness, maybe even excitement? How incredible that we have the ability to reverse engineer this process, to go into our subconscious and unlearn—unwire—these patterns.

If we are triggered by the fear or the unknown, it could be another clue. Remember, a clue refers to a chance to better understand something that is often a mystery to us. When we are triggered, blaming the person who is triggering us or making us angry can be a lot easier than looking at what is happening inside us. This isn't surprising, because we have covered up our pain. By avoiding pain and pushing it down, we can't see that pain is what lies beneath our fear reaction—when we're burying our heads in the sand, silencing our needs, or yelling at a child or parent, for example.

Merriam-Webster defines the adjective "triggered" as being "caused to feel an intense and usually negative emotional reaction." Enter our automatic reaction, a result of the pattern we've wired into our subconscious to protect us from pain. This very reaction, however, prevents us from being able to see what's beneath the mask of fear we are experiencing. Are we angry? Shameful? Jealous? If we react with rage or judgment, we aren't able to see what's beneath the mask, what we really care about, what we're scared is being threatened, or what we're trying to protect. We share that in common with fear. We are both trying to protect us. But while the reaction might seem like it's protecting us from the pain, it's only disconnecting us from it—so it still impacts us emotionally, physically, mentally, and energetically. We might stay focused on the sensation of anger—digging in our heels about why we're right and the other is wrong—leaving us further from what we seek—which is connection and being seen. Or we might double down on the judgment—*How could they have canceled on me at the last minute?*—rather than having curiosity about what is going on with them, which also takes us further away from what we want—what's beneath the trigger.

THE INFORMATION BENEATH THE TRIGGER

Our emotional reaction is rarely about the other person. I actually think of everyone as mirrors—reflecting back to me what I need to see about myself. If I'm getting angry, it's not because another person is making me angry. Rather, something inside me is experiencing pain or fear or anger, which is easier than sadness and unknowns. Why? Perhaps it goes back to the widely accepted story that vulnerability is weakness, or about the all-consuming pursuit of happiness. Thanks to neural plasticity, however, we can build a new neural pathway telling us that vulnerability is a strength.

There's a common misperception that it's easier to get angry or shut down than to feel what many consider messy emotions like sadness, shame, regret, or pain. My client interactions have shown me that feeling an emotion isn't the hardest part. Resisting feeling the emotion is. Our resistance to feeling what we feel may be one of the largest burdens we carry.

I would be remiss not to mention the great work of Louise Hay. In her 1984 book, *You Can Heal Your Life,* Hay explains how our beliefs and ideas about ourselves are often the cause of our emotional problems and physical maladies and how, by using certain tools, we can change our thinking and lives for the better. Hay was able to put her philosophies into practice when she was diagnosed with cancer. She considered alternatives to surgery and drugs and developed an intensive program of affirmations, visualization, nutritional cleansing, and psychotherapy. Within six months, she was completely healed of cancer. She graced us with her gifts until her ninety-second year. I often reference her work, which brought to life the notion of "the words you use and thoughts you run create your reality." In order to identify the new thought pattern, Hay would begin with its probable cause, which was physically manifested through body parts, ailments, diseases, and so forth, and which she determined originated from fear. I believe fear causes dis-ease. If we don't attend to our emotional dis-ease, it can manifest into physical disease.

Fear causes stress. The Mayo Clinic speaks to the severity of stress on our health:

> The body's stress response system is usually self-limiting. Once a perceived threat has passed, hormones return to typical levels. As adrenaline and cortisol levels drop, your heart rate and blood pressure return to typical levels. Other systems go back to their regular activities. But when stressors are always present and you always feel under attack, that fight-or-flight reaction stays turned on. The long-term activation of the stress response system and too much exposure to cortisol and other stress hormones can disrupt almost all the body's processes. This puts you at higher risk of many health problems, including:

- Anxiety and depression
- Digestive problems
- Headaches
- Muscle tension and pain
- Heart disease, heart attack, high blood pressure and stroke
- Sleep problems
- Weight gain
- Problems with memory and focus

The stress response system underscores the importance of having a healthy relationship with how we engage our fears.

I admit, it can be challenging to practice the pause when we've been triggered—but it is possible.

We are the architects of our freedom.

If you feel your fear reaction building—tightness in your chest, a clenched jaw, ears getting hot—pause before it builds to the peak reaction: screaming at a partner, appeasing someone when you're out of capacity, storming out, or whatever your reaction is. The great news is it doesn't take nearly as long to unwire a pattern as we have spent wiring it. *Once we see something, we can't unsee it.* But it does ask us to practice differently.

One of my favorite patterns to work on unwiring is the incredibly common fear of the unknown, which starts at such an early age. Picture a child on their first day at a new school. They may hide in their bedroom closet before it's time to go or act out to avoid going at all. There are so many unknowns, and without knowing that these fears are irrational, a child's brain is reacting to the fear of the unknown the same as it would to a rational fear. Fearing the unknown is another misconception to me, similar to vulnerability being a weakness. What's one thing (experience or person) in your life that didn't initially come from the unknown? Nothing originally came from the known. How were we conditioned to fear the unknowns so gravely?

Fear is often learned early on in life, and this is something adults can be proactive about. When adults understand their relationship with fear, they can engage their children to establish relationships with fear at a younger age. You can begin by asking a child what the story is. What are they afraid of? There might be a painful experience they had that would benefit from some discussion about it. Then, what is true? What do they love that they might find there? What are they curious about? What might they learn they love? What are they excited about, even if it's wearing the new shoes they got for the first day of school?

And if that's not a doorway in, what's an "and" you can practice? How can a child's fear exist while you also create a world for them to redirect their attention to? Perhaps the tickle monster shows up five to ten minutes before it's time to go every morning and the car is home base. Then, perhaps initial questions of the morning can be revisited that evening, so they have a chance to connect with what was true, or not, about their fear.

WHAT ARE YOU AFRAID TO EXPRESS?

We have the opportunity to retrain our minds, whatever age we are. Think about what brings you joy. Learning? New flavors? New friendships? New experiences? When you travel, do you only return to places you've been? Now that you're practicing the pause, what new can you lean into when you've given yourself the option to choose differently? What new neural pathways do you want to form?

Recently I was working with a client on letting go and allowing things to unfold a little more naturally versus her previous approach of outlining all her professional and personal endeavors, often step-by-step, with every single step planned.

> *The cave you fear to enter holds the treasure you seek. Fear of the unknown is our greatest fear. Many of us would enter a tiger's lair before we would enter a dark cave. While caution is a useful instinct, we lose many opportunities and much of the adventure of life if we fail to support the curious explorer within us.*
>
> —Joseph Cambell

The next time we had a video meeting, after the session when we previewed a new strategy for her, I noticed a huge shift in her energy.

"You look different; how do you feel?"

"I feel at peace."

"What do you think is contributing to that?"

"I feel more in control. Letting go allows me to feel more in control."

Isn't that ironic?

If we look at anger as a specific data point, how can we mine it for information? After all, it's showing us that something important has been threatened or absent. We don't talk about healthy expressions of anger, leaving many of us without a way to explore them. But expressing anger is an excellent way to open ourselves to it.

PRACTICE

This practice may lead to tears, sadness, and even laughter. It's a release that offers one helpful step in eradicating the pain that might be stuck inside your body. Do you have anger to tap into and express? Here are a few ideas:

- Go to the ocean or a natural body of water and scream into the waves.
    - If you can (I live near the Pacific Ocean and it's cold, but I do it every time!), dive in after you scream and let the water wash you off.
    - If you're not near a large body of water, you can visualize this process by watching your anger flow away into the water.
- Take a boxing class or just beat the hell out of an innocent mattress.
- Go to the Dollar Store, buy some dishware, take it home, and smash it on the ground. I've even had clients make beautiful mosaics out of the shrapnel.
- Roll the windows down while you're driving and scream (not at someone else). Be sure to drive safely.
- Break out the crayons and color how you feel. Bonus points for swearing while you do it, using all the words that would've gotten you into trouble as a kid.
- Find an angry song that helps put words to your feelings and then bellow it at the top of your lungs.
- Write a letter to the person or whatever else you're angry at. Let it all out. Then find a safe place to burn the letter and let the anger go.
- What feels like a way of releasing for you?

Pent-up anger can contribute to unintentional emotional reactions. When we can release anger healthily, we can find or replace other reactions that don't serve us. Because anger is seen as negative and inappropriate to express, many of us might have some old anger stored in our system. Releasing it creates space—an example of how we can unwire old patterns that don't serve us while we wire in new patterns that do.

Rewiring is how we take the lessons from our fear and implement them through choices that enable us to build the life we want. My work has shown me a number of things. One element that I love is how similar we are to one another (we all share similar fears) *and* how different our experiences and stories can be (stemming from these very fears). There is no algorithm to doing the work needed to unwire old patterns that no longer serve, just like there is no magic weight-loss pill. There are practices and tools that can assist, but each person has their own unique journey.

Our life journeys are made up of our experiences and our societal, familial, and cultural insights and teachings. The evolutionary element of fear works to protect us from fear and pain through our journeys, no matter the cost. Fear is doing the best job it can do at its job—to protect us.

The more we understand our unique patterning, the easier it becomes to practice self-observation and know what practices might be protective mechanisms from old fears and pain and where our new fears might be inviting us today.

SEEDS TO PLANT

- The only way to navigate this journey is the way that resonates for you.
- Avoiding our pain only contributes to our protective patterning, which keeps us reinforcing the fear-based story.
- Feeling an emotion isn't the hardest part–resisting feeling it is.
- Once you see something, you can't unsee it.
- We can create a new neural pathway that invites the unknown with curiosity.
- The mystery of who we are, the mystery of how we really feel, is a mystery that wants to be solved, and anger is one of the most obvious clues it can send us.

CHAPTER 15

THE EIGHT BASAL FEARS REVISITED

To heal our wounds, we need courage to face them.
—Paulo Coelho

My belief is that fear can unite us. I actually think it's one of the most powerful emotions we have in common, right up there with love and hurt. Fear crosses all perceived lines that divide us.

Communities are based on commonalities. One of these commonalities is that we all have fears. If we had a healthy relationship with our fear, we could use it to gain more insight, to understand ourselves and one another. This understanding moves us away from a scarcity mindset—which is the greatest divider of all—and helps bring us together.

By understanding the information our fear has for us, we can gain increased access to what is true for ourselves. Our basal fear or fears (as some people have more than one) connect us to our greatest pain—what our fear is protecting us from and what we are wanting to heal. Thus, it becomes an access point to increase our freedom—to learn about what pain is hiding beneath the fear that is wanting to be healed.

HOW FEAR CAN HELP US HEAL OUR PAIN

One of my clients, whose mother was mentally ill, underwent a lot of emotional, verbal, and even physical abuse. She was often told that she wasn't allowed to do something, she wasn't worthy enough to do something, she wasn't important enough. She was never told she was loved. She was left to take care of herself for long stretches of time—sometimes having basic needs that wouldn't be attended to. Her basal fear is the fear of rejection.

Remember that the unintentional opening for the fear of rejection is to do anything to be accepted. The unintentional closing, on the other hand, is to say, "I'm not going to try." This was her modus operandi for decades. Asking her what she wanted wasn't a door in, because this pain and fear had made her believe she wasn't worthy of her wants. However, when we could use another door, we had room to explore. Rather than looking at what she wanted, we looked at how she wanted to feel. We used the mantra "Let's just check it out" to create a new neural pathway for her to explore. While her fear was protecting her from the pain she experienced while she was younger, it was also showing her exactly where she wanted to grow, to explore new things, to begin to connect to her worth indirectly through finding things she enjoyed.

The notion of being united through our basal fears wasn't a hypothesis I started with. Originally, I wasn't even looking at fear. Years back, in service to my guiding North Star to create a world of *and*, not *or*, I went in search of a framework for empathy. Much to my surprise, empathy led me to fear. When we are aware of and connect to what is true for ourselves, we can be more open to understand what is true for another as their truth does not invalidate our own. The challenge comes when we don't know what our truth is or haven't taken the time to connect to it: we can feel threatened by another person's commentary.

As a reminder, here are the Eight Basal Fears:
1. Loss (letting go)
2. Rejection (not being liked or accepted, abandonment)
3. Loneliness and isolation (fear of being alone)
4. Self-worth (not being good enough, failure, inadequacy)
5. Authenticity (not being one's true self, fear of success)
6. Feeling lost or directionless (fear of the unknown)
7. Scarcity (fear of not having enough)
8. Death/mortality (loss of self)

Remember, this is not to say everyone has all eight fears at all times in their life. You might have one or two that predominate. My core basal fear is lack of self-worth, and many of the issues I have had to work through in my life come back to it. You may have one or a few. And depending on what life circumstance you find yourself in, one of them may become relevant or timely for you.

Let's revisit a couple of possible unconscious reactions. We can react to fears unconsciously in two ways, with an unintentional opening or an unintentional closing. The opening may cause us to do whatever we have to in order to try to fill the void (pain) while an unintentional closing may cause us to shut down or, in some other way, take ourselves out of the equation. There is an unintentional opening and closing for each, so what it looks like might look different for each of us. By way of example, let's briefly consider self-worth.

Self-worth (not being good enough, failure, inadequacy):
I'm not good enough. . . . / There's something wrong with me. . . . / I'll never get it. . . .

Unintentional opening: *Therefore I'll overextend myself.*

Unintentional closing: *Therefore I'm stuck trying to compensate or medicate, or therefore I'll shut down.*

In order to make this tangible, let's look at how this might play out in a relationship. When I'm coming from a mindset of lack while being in a relationship, playing out my fear of lacking self-worth, I might quiet my needs in order to appease the other person's needs. I might overextend to ensure that they're feeling taken care of and heard and seen—in fear that if I do have needs, I might be a burden. Alternatively, in order to prevent possible pain, if my needs aren't being met and we're not in a place of balance or reciprocity, I might walk away before trying to have a conversation to address this imbalance because I fear the outcome. My walking away then protects me from having to face this fear. However, these unintentional openings and closings further perpetuate these very fears.

WHAT INFORMATION DOES YOUR BASAL FEAR HAVE FOR YOU?

Let's look at another example, one where someone used his fear to create the most intentional experience he could—for the end of his life. One of the basal fears, and one that many humans share, is the fear of death. I had the gift of witnessing the most courageous choice, one that challenged what I knew to be possible about the journey to one's death.

Assisted suicide was legalized in 2018 in California. Due to severe health conditions, my dear friend Kelly selected his death date, just one and a half months shy of his seventy-sixth birthday. There is great emphasis placed on birthdays and their genesis: nine months of planning, honoring, and preparation in order to welcome life. Birthdays have become one of our key identifiers. What form can you fill out that doesn't require your birthdate? Yet how often do we think about, speak about, or even consider our death date? It's not that common. In fact, most people won't even talk about what death means to them and how they want to prepare for it. It's too scary.

Asking me to be a part of this day brought up fears for me too, as Kelly was part of my chosen family and this was the biggest ask that had ever been made of me. He was our neighbor when my ex-husband and I lived together, and we shared countless meals, movie nights, conversations, tears, laughs. Could I watch someone I care for this much die? What if it wasn't a gentle death? Would I ever be able to let go of the image? What if it impacted me and I couldn't show up for him as I wanted? I knew that I loved him. I knew he asked me to be there, and I knew that more than any of these possible but unprovable what-ifs, I wanted to hold my friend in love for his final breath.

It was years of pain and heartache and multiple ailments that led to this circumstance being considered a possibility. In the lead-up to his determined date, we reminisced, talked about pain, his gift of piano (he was a trained classical pianist), and what we were grateful for. We cried and laughed and recognized how he had a choice, given the circumstance, about how he wanted not only the end of his life to unfold but the lead-up to it. By turning into what he was afraid of, he was able to connect to all the elements he wanted to cherish on his way out: how he wanted it to be a celebration, what he wanted the last day to look and feel like, what I would need to be able to be a part of it.

And talk about a celebration. The last four weeks of his life were spent in community, with music nights, dinner parties, and one-on-one visits. It was a revolving door of connection, with great meals and spirits, libations, and moods—and the emotions of the impending reality—the closing bow—all existing simultaneously. At times, the impact of connection (weight gain, color in his face, joy being had) almost made some of us and perhaps Kelly as well question why he would be going through with this. But he knew, as did all of us, this couldn't last. He and I talked about what was to follow this choice, at which time he shared with me that he didn't believe there was anything following this life, that death was the end.

When May 7, 2018, Kelly's death date, arrived, we sat before each other in the morning with smiles across our faces, watery eyes, and a love so palpable you could feel it. We thanked each other for the love we shared, and recognized the courage Kelly had shown until this point and what this day would ask of him. He then told me that due to our conversations, he'd shifted his stance and while he may not have known exactly what was next, he was open to something being beyond his death, that this may not be the final ending. Goose bumps poured down my body, and a sense of peace enveloped us both.

Kelly's day was full of everything he knew would make him feel complete—a "parade" down Fillmore Street to his daily stomping ground (Peet's Coffee), songs sung by local artists including "When You're Smiling," hugs and well wishes by all his community, and his final meal (pancakes and vanilla ice cream with dulce de leche).

He had asked four of us—Dave, his stepdaughter, a friend, and me—to be with him in his final moments—to hold space for his end-of-life transition. The music began: Scriabin, recorded by Kelly from years prior. We mostly sat in silence, sometimes we expressed love, embracing with our eyes closed or gazing into the souls of one another.

By law, Kelly had to administer the cocktail himself. Even prior to taking the cocktail Kelly was fading in and out. And even during the moments that I wondered if he would make it to the time of the cocktail, his eyes closed—his fingers still playing along with the music on his thighs. He committed much of his life to his love, the piano—and watching his joy while he was being called home as he was washed over with his passion was simply humbling. Talk about living your why.

When the final stage was upon us, he looked at each of us, spoke to us directly, telling us exactly what he was grateful for: that he loved us and that because of our love for him, he could do this. That he was at peace. It was time.

The final song, "Nocturne ('Into the Night',)" by Chopin, commenced. He poured orange juice into a glass, mixed it together with the medication, and sipped the straw until it was gone. . . . He had one to two minutes to drink it. He did it in ten seconds. We raised our shots of tequila and toasted Kelly one final time. He sat back against the couch, a childlike grin upon his face. "I did it." Even he surprised himself with his courage. As he closed his eyes, we all continued to convey our love and hold him. Within minutes after one extended inhale and exhale, Kelly made his closing bow.

We sat in silence. We shared love and connection through our eyes. We embraced one another and we cried. This was the most courageous and gracious I've ever witnessed a human being. It was everything, but more than anything—it was beautiful. And Kelly, as we knew him, was no longer. Tears of everything.

This day required courage at every moment from all involved. No greater than Kelly, who chose to be his most courageous self again and again—without hesitation. To dress and approach the day with a smile and gratitude, to be carried down to the parade of his life, to connect with person after person at his communal celebration, to have his last meal, take the antinausea pill, follow his planned closing (Chopin), to take the cocktail, to begin his transition in love, with love . . . in peace.

Kelly was able to create the final experience he wanted in his life and conduct his closing bow with the intentionality he did because he went directly into his fear to see what it had to share with him. And he wanted piano, community, and a peaceful moment of transition. As a result, it was the most intentionality I've ever witnessed around a death. There was immense love and connectedness and holding as he embraced the biggest fear of life, because he was able to connect to what was most important and then close the gap by moving into his courage.

What a model of courage and grace. These are the gifts I will gratefully carry on from that day with Kelly. It was more important for me to hold my friend in love and peace as he took his final breath than it was to allow any what-if scenario I may have been running in my head to dictate my choice. My being able to turn into my fears and apply my courage to be there every step of the way with Kelly enabled, for me, the opportunity to heed his teachings about peace.

WHAT INFORMATION DOES YOUR BASAL FEAR HAVE FOR YOU?

I believe that the way through begins with the way in. Shadow work (exploring the darkness that has been associated with fear) is one way in. My hope is that, in time, when the shadows appear, you may be able to greet them with levity. *Oh, you again? What are you here to show me? What am I not looking at? Where am I wanting to grow?* It may feel aspirational in this moment, and it creates a possibility for a new way forward—one with more freedom.

I encourage you to connect with what your basal fear or fears might be.

> ### REFLECTION
> Connecting to Your Basal Fear(s)
>
> While each of us may experience some of the unintentional openings and closings for each of the Eight Basal Fears, we often have a predominant one or two that we frequent the most.
>
> When we know what our primary basal fear is, we can begin to become aware of its presence and learn how to build responses to it instead of reactions.
>
> - Review the Eight Basal Fears.
> - Which reactions feel like the most commonly experienced ones for you?
> - Do you more frequently react by unintentionally opening or unintentionally closing?
> - How frequently do you experience this fear? Daily? Weekly? Get a sense of how much you are practicing (reinforcing a pattern) your reaction.

Fear is something we avoid experiencing and talking about but has so much information for us. Did I have fear going into that day with Kelly? Of course I did: for Kelly's experience, for myself and what I might see or feel, and for how the experience might impact me afterward.

SEEDS TO PLANT

- Our fears cross all the perceived lines that divide us.
- Exploring our fears grants us a greater understanding of ourselves and one another.
- We can move away from the mindset of scarcity.
- Ask yourself, *What is my relationship with my fears?*

CHAPTER 16

LISTEN TO LISTEN

Listening is about being present,
not just about being quiet.
—Krista Tippett

We are taught to speak, to read, and to write. We're not taught to listen. I find this fascinating. Listening is an art of its own. As such, I believe that people most often listen in order to speak. There is a great difference between listening to speak and listening to listen. When we listen to speak, our brain, through confirmation bias, is actually looking for choice words to either support our existing stance or debate an opposing stance. Even in a conversation, we begin from a place of defense, judgment, and separation. Earlier, in Part 3, the notion of perspective spectrums was introduced. When we are in a place of judgment, we are not practicing curiosity.

When we listen to listen, we can release the attention of our opinions. Opinions, when relating to another's beliefs or ideas or previous personal beliefs, can be based on an assumption of knowledge. When we truly come from curiosity, we don't know what's possible, what's being said by another, or what might be true for our current self. When we're listening to speak, the inner voice we might be hearing (on a loop) may be coming from the belief we lodged in our subconscious about what we're not capable or worthy of. Looping means lodging. When we allow fear to run on a loop, we are lodging it into our subconscious.

LISTENING CAN FORGE CONNECTION

Listening to listen is the home of humility and the beginning of true connection, to ourselves and one another. When we seek to understand, we can access new and otherwise inaccessible thought forms and creativity as we gain new knowledge and insights. Listening to listen means listening without an agenda, which helps break down the misperception of what divides us.

This can be challenging as we were not taught to listen in this way. We weren't taught to listen at all. We didn't actively practice listening to listen, and whatever we practice becomes ingrained. As we've noted throughout, what we practice repeatedly become automatic reactions, which we're working on unwiring through this process.

One of my clients told me that he had received feedback from his boss, and separately his wife and daughter, that he wasn't a good listener. They told him that he often interrupted them and rarely engaged with the information they were offering; rather, he would repeat the point he was trying to make. He said he could see the impact it was having on people, which he wasn't pleased about, but didn't know how to listen differently. We brought his awareness to what he was experiencing in these moments and what cues his body was giving him, becoming impatient or digging his heels in about the point he wanted to make.

Here's the practice I gave him to start listening more actively. First, he needs to identify his desired outcome—how he wants to start behaving instead of how he is currently reacting. Then, he needs to identify what his cues are that are triggering the automatic reaction, so that he can bring his awareness to when to pause and how to engage that moment differently—to ensure he's behaving how he wants to be:

Desired outcome: Shifting from listening to speak to listening to listen.

Notice your cues:

- The feeling of "Let's move" (insinuating impatience: he thinks the person should wrap up what they're saying, or that he's ready to leave the conversation).
- He experiences what he describes as a "turn in my belly."

PAUSE

Remember: You cannot be judgmental and curious at the same time.

- Allow yourself to let go of your agenda (I promise you won't forget it).
- Even if you are skeptical, let your skepticism become your discernment.
- Get curious: What are they offering? You may either shift your opinion, or it will give you more insight as to what's most important about this for them.

> **PRACTICE**
>
> Now it's time to bring your self-awareness to how you are listening.
> - When you listen, what state are you listening from?
> - If you let go of any previous story or agenda, what are you curious about now, when breaking apart an old story?
> - When speaking with another, what are you curious about? What did you learn by being in conversation with them?
> - What was hard for you as the listener?
> - What does it feel like to be listened to?

LISTENING ALLOWS FOR NEW PERSPECTIVES

The other gift of listening to listen is the access to space it provides. When we're listening to speak, the moment any space presents itself (a breath, the end of a sentence), we're jumping in to fill it—think of how rapid-fire the self-critic is when it's on a loop. *Silence is powerful and often holds rich information.* See what arises in moments of silence—both in conversations with yourself and others.

I find this form of listening to be the seat of true deepening, of intimacy, or of seeing another person fully and seeing ourselves more truly. *Being seen is one of the most powerful gifts we can experience.*

After twenty-three years of mostly being estranged from my father, he returned on a pivotal day of my life. Prior to that pivotal day, I had left my marriage pretty abruptly. A couple months after my marriage ended, I would return to the apartment where I had lived with my soon to be ex-husband and retrieve my things. I had asked my mom, brother, and sister-in-law to help me. When I arrived, not only were the three of them there, my other brother and Dad (who I hadn't told of this situation) were there as well. Everyone was there to support me. There wasn't time or space for me to process my dad being there, so we got to it—together.

It was a full day. Most everyone stayed through to the evening to help finish as much as we could. And the next day, my dad returned home. I had been through years of therapy and a variety of alternative healing modalities to work through the painful experiences my dad and I had been through—which led to my pain, my anger, my guilt, my disbelief, my lacking self-worth, and so on. I had finally gotten to a place where I had forgiven myself, which was actually what enabled me to finally forgive him even before he had returned that day, though he wasn't aware of that. My forgiving him at that time was for my own healing.

So I had a choice. Did I want to meet the man who is my father? To learn who he is? As a man, not as the father that I had as a little girl, and who I no longer needed.

He is, after all, a huge part of who I am: because of his genetic influence, his role as a father in my young years, and the impacts of his absence, which truly served as a gateway to my self-discovery, through the shadows. I decided the answer was yes.

I no longer had an agenda. I had already said goodbye (internally) many times to him. So we began again. I listened to understand who he was, what beliefs he subscribed to, what he wanted for this lifetime, the world, the planet, how he practiced his practices.

My father is a spiritual being. Because of our experience when I was twelve, I shunned spirituality for years as it represented abandonment to me. This was probably the beginning of my connecting to my ology, which I outlined in the introduction. Much to my surprise, while I was anti-anything spiritual, over the years I would often find myself in settings with exposure to spiritual practices. Denying my own spiritual beliefs to myself back then, I began to decipher what resonated with me, what triggered me, and what wasn't meant for me. I was skeptical about all of it. But over time, my skepticism became my discernment.

My ex-husband is a good man with an incredible heart, and I'm grateful to count him as a friend today. But when we were married, we were not a healthy fit. While we only ever wished the best for each other, we didn't always bring out the best in each other. Another fear that had kept me in the marriage was my fear of being alone, a huge fear of mine at that time. When I left, part of it was coming from a place of owning my worth. It felt like coming full circle to reunite with my dad at the time when I took my power back. This would become the beginning of opening to greater healing than I imagined. It was also when I began actively exploring my remaining shadows and discovered what was true for me as an energetic being.

While listening to my dad from a place of curiosity, I could learn about myself—the elements we shared, where we differed—and I could honor those differences. I could learn from his experience and wisdom. I could let him be him. From that place, I could also share who I was. Today we have a new way to be in relationship with each other. We can see each other for who we each are. It's a relationship I'm not sure we would have had if we didn't go through the darkness, together, apart. And, wow, did this journey inform so much of my beingness.

Listening to listen . . . what a beautiful invitation to deepen connection to ourselves and one another.

SEEDS TO PLANT

- We're taught to read, speak, and write, not to listen.
- Listening to listen is the home of intimacy, being seen, and connection.
- The power of silence is rich beyond measure. What does the silence hold for you?
- Remember: Silence is where inspiration is received. Feeling uninspired? Be quiet for a second. Maybe your muse is trying to get a word in.

CHAPTER 17

LET'S CLOSE HOW WE BEGAN

There's nothing in a caterpillar that tells you it's going to be a butterfly.
—Buckminster Fuller

There are a lot of reasons to get curious about fear, but mainly, because we fear fear, we often allow it to prevent us from turning toward it to reap the information it has for us. When we do, it becomes the door opener for the very change we are seeking.

We tend to focus on what fear has prevented us from doing. What if we consider these other perspectives? What has fear made possible for us? What did fear cause us to do?

Our fears partly make us who we are. Thank them for what they have brought us and are bringing us. Fear is constructive and useful, if we can be thankful for it and explore the data it has for us. Reframing our relationship with fear and changing our perspective opens the door to being our authentic self by allowing our brains to choose what we are trying to create intentionally as opposed to running from that which we are trying to protect ourselves.

Fear reveals our deepest values. When things like anxiety, insecurity, sorrow, shame, anger, comparison, or competition, for instance, appear as masks of fear, we are alerted that one of our values isn't being honored. Whatever that value is, fear points us toward what we're in service of, what matters most. Fear can be our flashlight, illuminating the path to purpose for our courage to walk.

Every moment, person, and experience we come across can serve as mirrors—reflections of our true selves or what's standing in the way of being our true selves. These moments and people provide us the pathway to continually becoming the next best version of ourselves. In my ideal scenario, and as I've witnessed with so many others, we never reach an end state. Each of us is continually evolving.

A victim mindset causes stagnancy and disempowerment while a growth mindset enables us to stand in our power. A victim mindset is one that practices a mindset of lack: *Why is this happening to me?* This framing perpetuates lack and scarcity. However, if we consider, *Why is this happening for me?* it becomes an opportunity, even if it's a challenging circumstance. The opportunity is for growth as opposed to victimization often looking for another to blame—a process void of growth, resilience, and personal power. Being a prisoner to a mindset of lack is a challenge in itself. It's the kind of difficult that begets more hardship. There's no way through. It's a cycle of lack.

Let's Close How We Began

Growth can be hard but has a rewarding outcome. We can break the cycle and create new paths forward in service of building the life we want, supported by intentional ways of being. It may not be the easy way until it becomes the simple way of being. Be patient with the process, allow the body to do its work, and support yourself with love and the knowledge that everything is changing all the time.

Again, nothing is better at doing its job than fear. As we step out of our comfort zone and make a change, our fear is going to get louder. This is because when we remain the same, staying in our comfort zone, fear knows how to protect us. However, when we step outside our comfort zone and practice new ways of being, fear doesn't yet know how to protect us. It's a good thing that courage can help close the gap. Courage isn't the absence of fear; rather, it's the transformation of energy.

I have shared an alternative perspective with you about fear. Thank you for taking this journey with me. I want to plant one more seed with you: While this book is focused on fear, it's truly about love. I love love. I am humbled by love of all kinds and am guided by its life force. Love in partnership with parents and friends and chosen family and siblings and strangers and self and nature and, and, and. . . . And I'm struck by its many faces—awe, gratitude, grief, abundance, hope. I often ask people what love means to them and rarely receive one common answer. It can range from kindness to loyalty to compassion to respect and many others. One particular response I received gave me pause. This particular person told me love was the ability to receive. I witness the challenge that many people have with receiving love—often, in part, I believe, due to their unexplored fears, their fear of rejection, self-worth, not being enough, and so on.

What if fear is love in disguise, an access point calling us in to learn about what love means to each of us? I know the rational conclusion might be to say that the opposite of fear is safety, but we have seen through many examples that what is keeping us safe may not be best for the most recent version of ourselves. We may even have the false perception that what we know is what is safe for us, and that safety may still be protecting us from past pain. My fear of abandonment asked me to find ways to love myself, to connect to my worth, and to find my wholeness within. Only then can I be open to the complement of healthy love with a partner, open to what makes another whole.

What's more, we cannot open to love without the risk of opening ourselves to pain, because when we open to love, we open to potential loss. And grief is loss. Grief is love. It is grieving the loss of a love—both what we may have had for someone or something, and for being received in love by them. We aren't taught that grief is love. Only the positive side of spectrums is reinforced, so unfortunately grief is one of the emotions that falls into the bad pain category. And because we and others around us fear pain, on top of the loss and love we're feeling, it's also very common to feel isolated and alone when in grief. I wonder if we were held in that time of grief and loss, if the love—even if in a different form than joyful love—wouldn't be as hard to navigate without the loneliness and isolation? Maybe this can be an invitation for you to be with your grief or the grief of those around you differently, to honor the love that was and how it helped make you who you are. If we can open up to the notion that when we open to love, we do risk pain, maybe it would prevent some fear. Maybe it would even welcome it, knowing that while in a very different form, grief is love. I will always risk pain for love.

A PEEK INTO THE MACRO

I find it interesting that most people are familiar with the word "bystander" and very few are familiar with the term "upstander." By leaving our fears unexplored, we have been bystanders to our own beingness. When we stand up into ourselves, we can support one another—a call these divisive times in our macro environment are demanding of us.

Are you familiar with the adage "hurt people hurt people"? Well, if we run from fear and we run from pain, there's a lot of people who currently are hurting out there and don't have tools or ways to be with that pain. And if given a channel to put it into, such as hate, it seems like a reasonable displacement to make—anything to free yourself from your pain. And when it can't be yours, generally it has to be someone else's—someone else's fault, someone else's pain.

It is easy to get pulled into the macro fears of our time. There are many, and they're palpable. When you notice your cues that fear is "on you," pause. Ask yourself, *Is this fear mine?* Fear can feel contagious, and it's common to take on fears that might not be ours in that moment. Come back to your micro moment. If you can build a healthy relationship with your fear on a personal level, it will be easier to navigate the larger macro fears. Understanding one another fears is also a bridge to conversation and connection. But first we have to understand our own.

FEAR AS OUR DYNAMIC TEACHER

The only place we can begin to identify and practice the changes we want to see in ourselves is right there: with ourselves. Fear is not the enemy, although it can be if we don't have a healthy relationship with it. When we do, fear is rich with information showing us what's most important to us—what value is being threatened and, consequently, drives us. We can either react to it unconsciously or respond to it consciously and move into greater choice about how we navigate our lives.

Are you ready to see the beauty of fear? What if, with our understanding that its true intent is to protect us, we can learn the language of fear within each of us so that we can be in relationship with it? Fear can be our ally and informer.

Most important is to remember that seeing fear as an ally is a practice. The pace isn't what's indicative of shift and growth. Any pace is appropriate as long as there is continued inquiry, because our evolution is constant. It's never done, and our fears continue to evolve with us to show us where to grow. That's why reframing our relationship with fears from enemy into ally is so valuable. They can continue to play the role of informer—leading us to gain the insights our fears have for us and become a more authentic person.

Here's a quick reminder for one way to access each gateway into creating your healthy relationship with fear.

> ## PRACTICE
> If you notice yourself experiencing fear, see which of the three gateways feels like an approachable way to turn toward in order to see what information fear has for you:
> 1. Curiosity (what information does the fear have for me?)
> 2. Gratitude (how is this fear serving me?)
> 3. Purpose (my why is bigger than I)

Fears evolve with us. They have to. It's wired into the amygdala in our brain. As I have developed my relationship with fear, fear itself has developed in turn. I find it to be more subtle now than it was when I began my work, perhaps to trick me into staying safe (ironic, I know). And when I notice it, I raise my eyebrow, smirk my lips, and honor it: *Ah, you again. It took me a moment to notice you. Thanks for showing me I'm on the right track.*

When it's really hard, other stuff is also happening at that very moment that you can bring your attention to. You can choose to pause and get curious about what you are giving your attention to at any moment. A basic way to regain your calm is to notice what's happening around you. Is the wind blowing leaves in the trees? Is a bird flying by? Can you take a deep breath? What can you be grateful for at this moment?

Are you willing to accept the invitation to romance the shadows and step into more intentional choices? Inner peace? Greater freedom? Your truest you is waiting for you. What are you afraid of?

SEEDS TO PLANT

- A mindset of lack begets hard for hard's sake. Growth invites hard for rewarding's sake.
- How do your fears inform what love means to you?
- How do you practice being an upstander—for yourself or for another?
- Fear is the bridge that unites us.

EPILOGUE:
NOT ALL WHO WANDER ARE LOST

Don't read this chapter yet.

Inevitably, we sometimes forget our moments of clarity and stray back to familiar and unwanted habits. When you wake up in the shadow of unprocessed fear, doing things you told yourself you wouldn't do anymore, and you want to find your way back to intentional living, read this chapter then. Let it help you find your way back.

And when you do, avoid the temptation to criticize yourself for wandering off the path. You just might find that wandering is a natural part of living intentionally—an opportunity to learn from your own inner autopilot—and a chance to develop an even healthier relationship with the part of you that's in charge when you're sleepwalking.

If this is you and you find yourself in this place, please turn the page for help on how to get you back on track.

If you're reading or rereading this chapter, it may mean that you've hit a rough patch. You committed to having a more intentional, conscious relationship with fear. You committed to living in choice rather than reacting subconsciously. You had a good run . . . and then something happened and now you feel like you've lost ground.

You're human. We all are. These times are richer than they may initially appear.

The first thing to remember is that growth and transformation aren't linear. They don't happen at the flip of a switch. This is a process, a cycle of death and rebirth. We go through cycles daily—think of sleeping and waking. After a night of sleep, we begin again. We go through cycles monthly. The phases of the moon. The rising and falling of the tides. Even a woman's menstruation cycle—that cycle of ovulating, shedding, and beginning again, without which human life would not be possible.

Every time we expand into the next version of ourselves, a previous form dies. That doesn't mean we lose every element of our former selves. We have the power to choose what we leave behind, what we take with us, and what newness we want to invite in. The point is that cycles are fluid, they're dynamic, and they're a cornerstone of growth and transformation.

Of course, when you're in the middle of a setback or the messy part of the cycle of transformation, you may not particularly feel like you're participating in a sacred process. It may feel more like a chaotic whirlwind of shit. That's okay. The point is that it can often help to remember simply that we're all in a cycle, that it's organic and natural, and you are by no means alone.

To help with that perspective, I am grateful to have sat down with a client—and a good friend of mine—who was willing to share his experience of falling off and returning to the path. The themes he shared with me are common to those I've witnessed with countless other clients, and they reveal a cycle of wandering off the path, waking up and realizing you've strayed off the path, and getting back on track.

To help illustrate these cycles, we'll dive into a couple of the examples my friend shared with me around weight loss and navigating hardship with his spouse. When I speak to his experience with weight loss, I reference Noom, which is a weight-loss program tracking and monitoring system. We'll start with a critical part of the process—the part that may have motivated you to crack open this book again—the inevitable experience of losing our way and giving in to unprocessed, subconscious reactions to fear and pain.

WANDERING OFF THE PATH

When my friend feels like he's doing well and he's living intentionally, he can observe himself sticking to certain habits and rituals. He's logging his food and exercise on Noom regularly, taking the time to meditate, regulating screen time, and seeing good progress in his weight-loss goals. Then something happens that knocks him out of conscious choice. Perhaps it's an excessive workload. Maybe it's a painful exchange with his spouse. And then, "Oh shit." Kill the lights. He loses the thread. It's like sleepwalking. He and many like him will go on autopilot, leaving all those unintentional habits and background tracks to steer us through our day rather than the carefully considered choices we would rather be making.

Then he's left to face the consequences of living out of choice: The weight starts to come back on, he avoids looking at himself in the mirror, or he realizes he hasn't made eye contact with his spouse in a few days. In short, he starts to experience the signs that he's disconnected from his intentional self, without yet realizing what's happened.

For many, there's this weird time lapse between the moment we get lost and the moment we notice we're lost. We wander, half asleep, from unintentional decision to unintentional decision. What makes this sleepwalking experience even more disorienting is that we likely don't realize we've left the path until long after we've left it. The first few pounds that come back on are easily explained away. "That was just a one-time indulgence." The last few arguments with the spouse weren't that big of a deal. "We were both tired after a tough day at work." Any number of safety mechanisms in place will help convince us, "This isn't a big deal. Don't overthink it. Nothing to see here!" Sometimes it's all too easy to ignore or explain away the first few clues that you're starting to wander.

The trouble is, the distance back to our authentic selves only increases the longer we wander off the path of true choice. And then, as my friend shared, one day, out of the blue, he'll see himself do something or hear himself say something that sounds like it came from a complete stranger. Something so "not me" comes tumbling out of us that it's a slap to our own face—the first noticeable sign that we're miles away from our authentic self.

I've heard other clients describe something similar—a desire to understand where this self-destructive behavior might come from. Is it an accident? Is it intentional? Is it avoidable? Is it inevitable? Or, worse yet, did we somehow choose to go off the path because, deep down, some part of us wanted to do so?

Fortunately, it's just the next part of the cycle—the "snap out of it!" moment.

A RUDE AWAKENING

If you've ever seen a movie in which a decent human transforms into a monster and then transforms back again into a decent human being, then you'll know exactly how my friend feels whenever he realizes, *Oh, shit. It's happened again.* Shock. Horror. Perhaps even a touch of self-loathing. And you're left to deal with the very real consequences of living unintentionally, ruled by a bunch of fear-induced reactions that somehow bypassed the parts of your brain that know better.

The feeling of shock and horror? That could be your Claires coming to the rescue. It could be your authentic truth that you have previously connected with screaming from within you to get through the fog. You can almost taste it—the distaste—in your mouth. Something is off. *Wake up.*

This awakening is asking us to look for clues. The trick is to notice the clues as best you can so that you can give yourself as much choice as possible in how you live. I encourage my clients to think out loud so that they can hear the stories that might be taking them off the path. The thoughts we use create our reality, so paying attention to those thoughts is really important.

STAYING AWAKE

Like every other organic process in the universe, living intentionally is a cycle of falling into and waking up from the shadow of irrational fear. Just like dreaming, the time spent sleepwalking is the time our subconscious selves get a chance to exert themselves and take us where they want us to go, and then we get a chance to exercise our conscious higher selves and go back to where we would choose to go.

Not many of us like the idea of falling asleep at the wheel. We'd like to live as consciously and intentionally as possible. The good news is, if we pay attention, we can avoid—or at least postpone—falling asleep. We can, when we have the intention and the energy to do so, exercise our power to choose what happens next and stay in control of our own story.

What are some of the clues my client notices when he's about to wander off the path? For him, it's things like forgetting to log his meals and activities, skipping the gym, or realizing he's told his third white lie to his spouse about how he's really feeling. Maybe it's seeing the tell-tale dishes in the kitchen sink the next morning after a late-night second supper to swallow his feelings, or next-morning Amazon purchase confirmations that tell the story of a lonely soul looking to fill the emptiness.

In my friend's case, he wouldn't necessarily choose to stop entering his weight and food intake into his app or hide his feelings from his spouse. Rather, it can sometimes be an unprocessed reaction to his fear that's influencing him in ways he can't tell. If something is buried beneath the surface that he's afraid to express, and if he chooses to avoid expressing it, that unexpressed truth (which has a life force all its own) will at some point assert itself and drag him back into the shadow world, the realm of unprocessed fears and unfaced demons, a pattern of unconscious reactions. There is irrational fear lurking—in cahoots with pain—that he's having a reaction to, and that fear has a lesson to teach that will not be avoided.

In relation to the weight loss, my friend may still feel fat—or not as thin as he'd like to be. He may feel it's too hard and can't keep it up. In relation to his spouse, he may fear that if he shows up fully in the moment, he's going to feel how strongly he doesn't want to be there.

He's going to feel things he's either not ready to feel or not willing to face. He may be afraid of the difficult choices and changes the truth might force him to make. He may be afraid of feeling his deepest feelings and where they might lead.

And if you begin to look in the wrong direction, those feelings of shame and pain and fear and desire—can all begin to swirl around and overtake you. It's as if we fall into a fog—a moment before the falling asleep, *Oh shit, it's slipping* moment . . . and then as slippery as it came on, we fall into unconscious behavior. Sometimes we don't even just fall into it. Sometimes we're dragged into that unconscious behavior by deeper feelings that cannot and will not be denied.

So what do you do when you feel yourself slipping into your next sleepwalking cycle? Once again, we're given an opportunity to just go with the unconscious reaction or to take a closer look at what's going on and choose our response. Do we let our subconscious take over for a while and see where that leads? Or do we try to stay awake and explore what our fear and pain are trying to protect us from? Quite often, we're dealing with fears that are trying to keep us safe from some perceived pain—even when experiencing that pain might be exactly what we need in order to evolve and grow.

THE "SAFETY" ZONE

The safety mechanisms that can take control of our decisions are ingrained so deeply within us, and they don't have our best interest in mind at all times. Remember, these safety mechanisms are in the business of keeping us in our comfort zone. They're how we're programmed to avoid fear and pain. It's like the failsafe mechanism in newer cars: the auto assist, the steering wheel that yanks you back in the lane to "keep you safe." However, in some cases, your vehicle may be taking you down a road you didn't choose. You know the stories you hear about people who drove into a lake because their car—their GPS (global positioning system)—guided them there? In those moments, we are no longer connected to our PGS (personal gut system).

This underscores the importance of distinguishing between rational fear and irrational fear. My friend didn't want to go down that path. He saw a road that his automatic guidance system didn't see. A moment comes when you acquiesce control to the autonomic system—you choose to let the driver assist take over. We are conditioned to do what's easy. Up until now, it's been easier to allow the safety mechanism to take over instead of saying, *No, I choose to go here.*

Yes, we all do it, and it's understandable because sometimes we are driving tired and don't have the energy to make another new decision. But we need to be aware that when we let go, an automatic system will readily take over.

GIVING OURSELVES PERMISSION TO WANDER

During a moment when we were talking, my friend exhaled and landed into a realization. "It's annoying. You're doing so well, and you can sense that you're starting to run on autopilot—and you really don't want to, but you're too tired or too scared or both to stay in choice. You know you'll get back to the path later."

An easy example would be to go off Noom for a couple days—because he's been able to stop and get back to it before. Or to keep things superficial with his spouse because they could get back to the harder conversation later.

It might even be a conscious decision to let go. There might be a moment right before veering off the road that feels like *Fuck it. I'm going to choose the wrong thing because I can. I'm going to have this pizza at 2 a.m. I'm going to work all night and only get three hours of sleep and triple up on the caffeine tomorrow.* It might even be accompanied with a wave of relief that you can just sleepwalk a little: to no longer be responsible, to abdicate choice, to be an object, not a subject of your life. As my friend so beautifully put it, "To go from struggling soul to empty plastic bag swirling in an eddy of wind."

In time you may awaken to some confusion—a sense of lostness. *Oh shit, I'm stuck in a dumpster with no arms and no legs. How do I get out?* Remember, identity requires transformation. We go through cycles of death and rebirth, again and again. Having a sense of choice and intention will also go through cycles of death and rebirth.

If we feel like we're wandering off the path, we may be in a fluid part of the cycle. Just as driving drowsy is dangerous, we can choose to pull over and take a nap. You too can choose to clear some space. For me personally, space is where I allow my faith to rest. I may not understand this part of the cycle or love the patience it asks of me, and I am shown time and time again the value of space that cycles bring. For example, I might have an intention of changing the way I engage with people—where my needs get to be part of the equation. The space is the time between my noticing and communicating it and then seeing if I can be met differently. The space is where I trust that this person will either be able to support me as I'm wanting to be supported or will show me, for whatever reason, that they're unable to do so. In this case, my work doesn't have to do with the outcome. It is actually about letting go of the outcome and knowing that my focus is to speak to my own needs and hold my boundaries; that's my work. If I can stay true to that, the space will show me if I can move forward with that person or if it's time to make room for someone or something else. This is where our energy returns, where insights from our learning and growth inform the next version of our self.

If you're falling asleep, pull over. It's not such a terrible thing to slip occasionally into this state of choicelessness. Just don't get engaged or married, buy a house, or make other life-changing decisions when you're asleep. In fact, most heavy machinery comes with a warning not to operate if tired.

When you wake up, you might be disoriented. It might not feel natural. You might feel like, *Oh shit, what happened?* Typically, what wakes us up is the stench of unintended consequences. He stopped paying attention to Noom and put on twenty-five pounds. He cheated on his partner. He's not sleeping at night. We realize we've gone too far off the path. Fortunately, flowers grow in manure. There's always a blessing to find—and you'll find your way back to the road.

SO, WHAT DO I DO NOW?

Step one in any movie in which someone wakes up and they don't know where they are (the film *The Hangover* is a great example) is to look for clues. Find the signs that you're waking up. Know and remember there is a road to get back to.

Where is the road? This is where it helps to have practices that bring you clarity.

Get your toolbox.

Put up your Post-it notes.

Find a compass if you can't find the road. You'll find the road if you start practicing your practices again. The tools—pause, nexting, getting curious, asking yourself what is true and what you are telling yourself is true, reorienting to your values and your why—helped you before and they will again.

Allowing for cycles gives us a way to move out of shame; the cycle is a necessary part of the process. When you can set down the shame from a place of understanding, you can recognize where you are. The tools help you feel empowered, the road begins to emerge, and you realize you're on it.

In addition to looking for clues about how to get back to the road, you're also looking for the green shoots of growth and positive change that this rebirth connects you to—the ones that had time to sprout and grow while you were sleeping, because the Universe needs time to interact with us. We need time to integrate change and growth. Think of a baker, allowing dough to rise, giving yeast the time to do its thing.

The daily use of our practices is the road.

When you've been out of it—not making conscious choices and decisions—you come back not only to potential complications, you also come back to blessings that take root while you're sleepwalking. Part of it might be recognizing you were meant to have a little nap.

The more familiar you are with your cycles, the less scary they become and the more naturally you can come in and out of them with intentionality. Finding the path again isn't always easy, but your tools and practices will serve you well.

If we can learn to honor the cycles of death and rebirth, particularly when it comes to intentional living, we will give space to the growth and transformation that are alive within us.

ACKNOWLEDGMENTS

Ma, for teaching me what's possible when you say, "Yes, we can do that," for forging the path of what's possible, for modeling unconditional love.

Alexis Ryon-Melcher, for being a member of the initial offsite where it all came together. For your professional, humble, opinions (sage wisdom). For your unwavering commitment to peace.

Milly Mocodean, for being a member of the initial offsite where it all came together. For your commitment to unlearning. For the rocking chairs.

Josh Reynolds, for being the ultimate door opener in my life. For your continued support and respect. For your commitment to conviction.

Brandon Maslan, for your reflection redirecting me from empathy to fear. For your passion of empathy. Boom.

Alexander Margarite, Terri Burden, Wayne Lin, and Sophia Dai, for being the original sources of the term "mascots of change."

Denise Lucy, for your leadership, your poise, and your passion and commitment to betterment.

Mark Bockley, for connecting me to Thoth, for bringing the magical wisdom of Dagara to so many, for opening this gateway for me.

Acknowledgments

Dad, for being a significant teacher. What we have navigated through this life has given me more lessons than I could have ever imagined.

Graham Brandt, for being a pillar in my life. For modeling how a good human shows up to this life.

Darcie Abbene, my editor at HCI, for your guidance and support from day one.

And the team at HCI and Simon & Schuster, including Christian Blonshine and Larissa Henoch. Also thanks goes to Corinne Moulder, Madison Scheuer, and Smith Publicity Inc, for being my partners and publicists through the journey.

John Geoghegan, for your guidance and knowledge that helped realize this dream, from your editing to your recommended approach and holding me through the process.

Erika Leder, for being my first unofficial editor, for your guidance and your laughter.

Talia Brandt and Michel Narganes, for your legal guidance and support along the way and for being two badass women who model strong leadership.

Emma Flores, for your artistic gifts. For embracing the *and* of this life. For partnering with me in such a generative way and for being plagued with purpose.

To those I want to mention and thank for your support: Robyn Awend, Kennedy Brandt, Kate Courteau, Britta Cross, Leigh Ferrara, Rosemary Garrison, Camelia Gendreau, Lasse Green, Peter Guagenti, Sharon Harrison, Caitlin Kolb, Marley Moon, Annie Massoka, Erin Moses, Corey Norrell, Sunok Pak, Annie Rosenberg, Brac Selph, Dave Tighe, Kari Woldum, and Alex Zak.

For all my clients for showing up as active participants in your life and for being my teachers and inspiration.

Luna and the Universe, for always having my back—even when I may not have seen it that way . . .

NOTES

1. Rozycka-Tran, J., P. Boski, and B. Wojciszke, "Belief in a Zero-Sum Game as a Social Axiom: A 37-Nation Study," *Journal of Cross-Cultural Psychology* 46, no. 4 (March 19, 2014): 525–48, doi:10.1177/0022022115572226. S2CID 145451071.

2. Kozlowska, K., P. Walker, L. McLean, and P. Carrive, "Fear and the Defense Cascade: Clinical Implications and Management," *Harvard Review of Psychiatry* 23, no. 4 (2015): 263–87, doi:10.1097/HRP.0000000000000065.

3. Clayton, Ingrid, PhD, "Caretaking and People Pleasing Through the Lens of Complex Trauma," *Psychology Today*, March 24, 2023, https://www.psychologytoday.com/us/blog/emotional-sobriety/202303/what-is-the-fawning-trauma-response.

4. Clark, C., C. C. Classen, A. Fourt, and M. Shetty, *Treating the Trauma Survivor: An Essential Guide to Trauma-Informed Care* (New York: Routledge, 2014).

ABOUT THE AUTHOR

Guryan Tighe is an experienced leadership coach, workshop facilitator, and communications strategist whose clients describe her as a "fear technician." She founded her company, FOURAGE, on the belief that understanding and working with our fears, rather than trying to conquer them, yields more professional success and personal fulfillment. She's served in several roles over the years to enhance interpersonal relationships, leadership development, and organizational change, including serving as a chief culture officer and workshop facilitator. She also has experience in influencer relations, messaging and positioning, and internal communications. In addition to coaching a private clientele, Guryan continues to educate senior executives and help them reorient their relationship with fear as a recurring speaker with the Stockholm School of Economics Executive MBA Program and a trainer and executive coach at Dominican University of California's Institute for Leadership Studies through its Office of Executive Education.

A NOTE FROM THE ILLUSTRATOR

WHY I WAS CALLED TO THIS WORK

This invitation felt like kismet. I met Guryan through my tattoo client Alex, whose sleeve was inspired by her mentoring. Like Guryan, I'm "plagued by purpose" and driven by the fear of not making a positive impact. I'm drawn to her work because it rethinks how we handle discomfort.

Fear feels like a private club in which everyone's a member. In a world ruled by fear, it's no wonder we gloss over our flaws and hide our quirks. I've had a lifelong subscription to *Self-Judgment Weekly*, covering my anxiety, grand ambitions, hidden flaws, and perfectionist meltdowns. I'm here to level up in this fear-fueled quest, one existential crisis at a time.

A LITTLE MORE ABOUT MY ART AND PROCESS

I'm captivated by human emotions and connections. Growing up in an artist family, I learned to use art for curiosity and reflection. My goal is to create art centering empathy and understanding, especially across racial experiences. I started tattooing because it uniquely builds community and offers more than just aesthetic adornment. It's a sacred practice providing belonging and care in a world that often overlooks these needs. For me, tattooing is all about collaboration and healing.

I work in a private LA studio within a queer femme-run healing arts collective, alongside acupuncturists and body workers.

With gratitude,
Emma Flores (they/she), intentional tattooer and visual artist
Memoryinscriptions.com